Inspired Right.

simply better for everyone

Main Street Pilot

Inspired Right.

Copyright © 2016 by Main Street Pilot

All rights reserved. No part of this book may be reproduced, scanned, or distributed in any printed or electronic form without permission.

Library of Congress Cataloging-in-Publication Data
Main Street Pilot
Inspired Right. Simply better for everyone.
First Edition: December 2016

Cover Designed by Main Street Pilot
Book Designed by Main Street Pilot
Printed in the United States of America
ISBN: 978-1-682-73885-6

For information contact:
Main Street Pilot
13330 Noel Road
Suite 1100
Dallas, Texas 75240
+1.800.798.1955
http://www.MainStreetPilot.com

An opportunity to become
inspired by Right.

To Everyone

The pursuit of satisfaction through positive change and Better is a need that does not go away throughout our lives. Better is not always easy to accomplish, and sometimes we give up without trustworthy help or solid guidance. Thanks to all who have come before us who demonstrated a passion for supporting the pursuit and achievement of Better.

Please know that every effort our group makes to contribute to the positive, honorable pursuit of Better is rooted in our deep commitment to marginalize and stamp out Wrong and the life-limiting effects of Worse for everyone. Special thanks to those vested in resourcing the needs of the Main Street Pilot team as we worked to solve for a new Better and the completion of this book.

Your tolerance, patience, objectivity, encouragement, and trust were essential to our successful pursuit to debunk Wrong and activate our Right.

Your support allowed us to remain centered on the notion that untapped, attainable Better is out there in abundance and with the right tools and guidance Better is increasingly possible. And thanks to you, our readers.

Become inspired by Right and never value the pursuit of Wrong ever again. Stay steady in the perpetual need for Better and don't ever settle for Worse.

Inspired Right.

Got Better?

Introduction

With so much anxiety, anger, and divisiveness in our day it can be difficult to focus on improving things for ourselves and within the work or social groups that we move among.

Being successful at getting to what is better for us personally, in relationships, and in our communities at the different stages of our lives with the additional pressures of knowing we are going to make someone else mad or unhappy with what we say about what we want to do is a real challenge. This troubling condition can and must change if we want Better.

Despite our hyper-opinionated approach to communicating and picking sides today, we have seen a widespread and surviving undercurrent that we can do better, that Better is out there somewhere. It is tough to be hopeful but somehow our individual and collective hope survives.

Today, we have lost our ability to come together and to honorably pursue Better. We think that moving in a direction of positive change today is possible if we can figure out how to make it happen with an ability to satisfy the true desires of each person along the way.

A Better today is a complex puzzle. That is until we get to the root cause of our behavior. Getting to Better personally and collectively happens when everyone is standing on the same foundation and when everyone is using the same primary source of guidance to shape our thinking, decisions, and actions.

Something to bring us all together while completely respecting and honoring our individuality. Simply enough, that foundation is our sense of Right and that guidance source is using this sense as a priority compass in all that we do, the Compass of Right that we all have.

Our book takes you through some of the discoveries along the way to solving the puzzle of today's Better. We have been able to set the record straight in some key areas including our reliance and valuing of Wrong, uncovering surprising and valuable common ground for everyone, our misdirected selfishness about our lives and setting our objectives.

It is awesome how easy Better can truly become if we are honest with ourselves and respectful of others. Throughout the book there will be suggested times to take a few notes and we provide a simple exercise at the end of the book to help you define your Better and to start to see where a compass that utilizes Right, when used regularly and applying its guidance liberally, can make the success of Better possible and inspirational.

If you are not happy or are discouraged today, you may have Right all wrong. Getting what may guide you to point only at your Better can make life as inspirational as we all believe it was designed to be.

¤ ¤ ¤

Contents

Your New Right 17

Defining You Right 31

Obstructing Better 49

Compass of Right 75

Right In Common 103

Applying Right 123

More About Right 163

Part One

Your New Right

Something New

Much of what we bring to the conversation of Right is going to be new or different for many people. Our cultural conditioning has us in certain ruts and on certain tracks where Right has no place of prominence or reality. Right as an inspirational source in our lives is something new or something we lost an ability to use or rely on a long time ago.

Culturally we have reduced Right to a nice thought, "Do the right thing." Not that this phrase is a bad idea, but Right is not a priority in our thinking, our decisions, or our actions. It is fair to say that the idea that there is more in Right for us than Wrong is laughable today. Success, popularity, winning, and volumes of stuff cannot possibly come from Right. If you believe this about Right, you have it all wrong.

More about Right will show that life is not a burden by design and that when working with Right properly and honorably, our own sense of Right, that the burden becomes how to manage the opportunities
ahead of us that represent true satisfaction and joy. Our own sense of Right also comes with some uneasiness about selfishness.

Right is an enabler of Better individually first, and collectively almost by default the more we rely and trust its voice of direction.

Our own sense of Right cannot know the Better of others the way it knows our own.

Do not think about the Better of others for a little while. In fact, we found that by prioritizing the Betters of others above our own caused a lot of self-inflicted wounds in the form of living in a condition of Worse or carrying a constant sense and weight of regrets. Purposely not putting others before ourselves as a positive thing is new thinking and will be counterintuitive for many.

You may agree by the end of this book that your prioritizing of Better is upside down. We had life all wrong until we revisited our given sense of Right.

¤ ¤ ¤

Enter Right

Defining Better with real clarity is not possible without relying on the guidance of Right. When we include Right as an essential consideration, our chances of achieving positive change improved almost immediately.

Your Better is the same as any other goal or objective that we work towards and if it is not clearly defined we will never get there successfully. How we define our Better must align with our own sense of Right.

We learned that the sense of Right, which we all have, is the one source of guidance, a true compass, that could clearly show us where to go if we gave it the appropriate amount of time to help us. Your Compass of Right only points towards Better.

As you understand the process of activating or reactivating your sense of Right, you may experience some immediate direction. You may also have to wait and keep checking the compass and waiting for confirmation of the best path ahead. If we did not get a firm direction right away we knew this might be important enough for us to slow down, keep asking, and wait for the right direction.

¤ ¤ ¤

Inspired Right.

The Currency Of Right

The more we transact in life with Right as our compass the more we will find and enjoy its outcomes. What we use as "currency" to pass back and forth when using Right in our interpersonal exchanges, or transactions, is the currency of trust. When we are certain about our own foundations and principles and these can be verified as trustworthy by both or all parties involved the outcomes are only Better.

Trust and trustworthiness are something new for most everyone and anyone relying on the tactics of Wrong to get what they want. When transacting wrong, the currency or currencies cannot be trusted. We see the currencies of wrong to be primarily guilt and fear. That is what we pass back and forth instead of trust and satisfaction.

Some have a sense of guilt after transacting wrong where they blatantly take advantage of someone else. Some are made to feel guilty if they don't transact wrong and try to apply Right, and some have a fear that they could have gotten more if they had transacted with more Wrong.

Guilt and fear do not instill trust. Would we buy what we are selling each other differently if all parties involved could be trusted? How would today's transactions change or would the trades of the past have gone differently if all parties were honest? What would a deal look like if the only goal was Better for all sides?

When we talk about trading, transacting, and deals we are not just talking business. We transact with those closest to us and those we are forced to transact with as people. People transacting interpersonally with an expectation of satisfaction.

Trading with the currency of trust as an extension of Right is the real opportunity to move toward and successfully arrive at Better.

¤ ¤ ¤

Success Factors

A successful pursuit of Better for anyone requires a few things to be in place. You may already be pretty good at this game of life thing and may find a minor adjustment to your foundation or your sense of Right as you read ahead. Most of us could use more than a few general tips to find out where we are today and where we want to differently go towards our Better.

In all cases, the number one requirement for success is to be honest with yourself about what is right for you and a true pursuit of Better in all aspects of your life. We tend to mostly downplay or ignore honesty in our culture because we don't think there is enough in it for our selfish selves. We think that lying to ourselves is fooling someone else or lying to others is right.

The next thing needed to successfully pursue your Better is a genuine interest in improving the outcomes of your life efforts. You know, working, studying, interacting with others efforts. Our outcomes are the classic choice of accepting and wallowing in Worse by prioritizing the Better of others or deciding without question that your Better as a priority is the only way to go.

Some see this as a commitment to being more keenly alive and not living as one of the walking dead - just aimlessly being pushed around by life. This choice comes back to personal honesty. If you cannot say with certainty that what should and could bring you the most satisfaction and joy in your life is important to you then you are not fully alive and this book will be extra helpful. Apathy is one spell we break regularly with an activated compass of Right.

If you can say with honesty that satisfaction and joy are your number one priority, then you will for sure improve your chances of Better. The next and maybe the most important life-success factor in our complex today is to put ourselves first. Not selfishly in the way you might first think, but selfishly in the sense of avoiding Wrong and Worse at all costs.

Whatever might be Wrong or Worse for you. Become selfish about a pursuit of Better. Become selfish about using the resources and time we commit to all the other non-Better-for-us-stuff differently and only if it helps us to improve or live more keenly alive. Right is how we can learn to do selfish without taking advantage of others. The foundation of Right and our inner sense of Right is what is right for us first.

One last thing on our "keys to Better success" list is a willingness to spend as little time or effort as possible looking backwards or trying to fix past regrets or stuff that anchors us to the old path of Worse. Exercising our sense of Right will have us filling our personal, professional, and community buckets with so much goodness and Better that there will be no room for Worse, which is the condition that Wrong delivers for us every single time. Buckets, you know, the different compartments of our day that we pour ourselves into.

Now, some of what you suspect that you need or don't have on our keys to Better success list may not yet make perfect sense or seem simple. Trust us. Your Better will make perfect sense and Right is really, really simple to activate and use differently in your life if you are not using it to its full capacity today. It all starts with an evaluation of where you are with your Better and committing to honorably pursue what is right for you.

¤ ¤ ¤

Compass Points

You may have noticed the compass point icons like this one that are highlighting certain questions earlier in the book. These are key questions we asked ourselves and those questions we think are important to help develop an active compass or sense of our Right.

These questions represent your "Compass Points", or life locators and indicators that can show you where you are today and at any point in a pursuit of Better. Checking your compass points will also show how well your decisions and actions are aligning with where your sense of Right wants to take you.

Only you can know the answer to your Compass Point questions. Your answers will help you to check your thinking, experiences, and honesty regarding a pursuit of positive change and Better. From our experience becoming inspired by Right is not the same for everyone. The concept or definition of Better is not the same for everyone.

The outcomes depending on what guides you in a pursuit of joy and satisfaction are not the same for everyone. Wrong and Worse are understood by everyone, but your Better is completely unique to you.

Inspired Right.

At the same time, an honorable pursuit of Better when guided by our sense of Right is the same fulfilling opportunity for each of us.

A Compass Point question example: Were you born to seek and find Better? Or were you born to seek to find and wallow in Worse? If your Compass of Right will point only towards Better, which direction are you facing if you have trouble answering these questions with certainty about what is right for you?

We're always going to talk from a position of what is Better for you. We'll ask you again to forget about Better for others for a little while. Better is becoming our primary purpose in life.

There probably are other purposes to life that merit recognition besides satisfaction and joy but we are wired to prefer Better. Better for ourselves. How we define Better and how we pursue it over time changes but our sense of Right along the way does not.

¤ ¤ ¤

Got Right?

Part Two

Defining You Right

Questions

Many of the questions we have in our lives come from a lack of knowledge or understanding. Our pursuit of answers can be a positive curiosity or the pressure of survival. Some of this wisdom can come from experience and some from what we see in others.

Answers to the toughest questions of the centuries include, "What is the meaning of life?", "What is the purpose of my life?". These are questions not even remotely possible to solve if you cannot or will not first define who you are, what you desire honorably, and what your Better looks like as a person, a professional, and a citizen.

Other common questions regarding our today include, "Why should I care?", "What's in it for me?", "Why am I so lonely, so dissatisfied, so unhealthy, so broke, so mad, so victimized?".

The answer to these questions are equally impossible to find without knowing who you are and placing some sense of value and importance on your unique individuality and determining your positive or negative sense of being alive.

¤ ¤ ¤

Only One You

Let's start with the "value of you" for a second. Like the Eifel Tower, the Crown Jewels, the winning lottery ticket, you are one-of-a-kind. An original. Who you are, and your own Better, is as rare and valuable as these examples and any number of other rare things that come to mind. If it is lost it is gone forever. It is to be cherished, protected, defended, yet shown around and displayed for others to enjoy. People should not be a commodity or a disposable resource unless they choose to be.

Each of us is as unique as a cake baked from a batter of ingredients found only in our own secret recipe. We are made up of a wide variety of ingredients and various amounts of components that include where we've lived, how we've lived, our influences, education, income, likes, dislikes, personal tastes, strengths, weaknesses, our color, traditions, motivations and more.

This is important because the millions, maybe billions, of possible combinations of these ingredients within the makeup of any one person absolutely guarantees unique, valuable, interesting scarcity. This is not the mindset of the average person whose lens shows burden ahead.

A lens spotted with the things that not only obstruct our view ahead it prevents others from seeing the uniqueness and value within.

Can our inner sense of Right, this Compass of Right change this condition? It can. Once we begin to focus on what is honorably right for us we can also start to see, appreciate, and respect what is right for others.

¤ ¤ ¤

Inspired Right.

All About You

Do you think that your life is all about you? Seriously. We know our lives involve others and the honorable pursuit of Better does not include preying on others. Do you think that your life should be all about you? Until we addressed this question satisfactorily ourselves, our lives did not have a prayer of achieving satisfaction.

Trying to define Better and who we are is pointless if we did not believe that life is the best thing that was ever given to us. We hope to help you successfully debunk any conventional thinking or the opinions of others as your source of defining you or inhibiting you from putting yourself first. Activating your sense of Right is the key.

"You first" means that you are going to become more self-reliant. More reliant on your own sense of Right and direct yourself to Better. Better does not include a subservient reliance on others. Refusing to put others before yourself if their expectations will prohibit your Better will also elevate the reality of honor and trust in all aspects of your life.

"Me first" made us uncomfortable because we had this other vague cultural topic gnawing at us that we know as selfish.

We hate to break the news to anyone offended by the idea of selfish but "your life" starts with the letters Y O U. Who can deny or argue this away if Better is the only acceptable destination for each of us and all of us?

¤ ¤ ¤

Defining You

What defines you? Our view is that your Better or Worse defines you. Nothing else. Shocking and counterculture, we know. Since I define my own Better or accept my own Worse, I define myself. When relying on my Compass of Right, how I honorably pursue my Better is who I am. That's it. Who are you? How easily can you answer that right now or before you define your Better? Who you are can be a really tough question if we don't know our Better or use our sense of Right.

We might answer before we understood Right to be our guide that who we are is a color group, economic group, sexual orientation group, gender configuration group, religious group, age group, or on and on. Nothing is further from the truth about our individuality.

Once we defined our Better, it revealed to us that all this other stuff our culture uses to group us is just window dressing. All the effort, arguing, debating and divisiveness that we thought could help us stand out and be recognized makes us less identifiable as individuals once under the tarp of a generalized group. We choose to blend into vagueness if we insist on being identified by a group or the sides we pick in our personal, professional, and civic lives.

If I am defined by the group I pick or by an outward appearance, how can anyone see the real me? Who decides what Better looks like for each of us within the group we pick or are put into by others? Pick a side or be taken advantage of is the rationale today to avoid becoming marginalized.

The reality is that the more groups that we pick not aligned with the pursuit of our Better means we will be taken advantage of instead of being protected. By the way, our own Better is not as militant as group Better. It doesn't have to be.

If who you are is what fascinates you, inspires you, and aligns with a distinct interest in Better as a priority you won't need a safe zone to say it or sanctuary zone to hide in. Who you are may include character traits like kind, happy, smiley, grumpy, patient, impatient, tall, short, slim, otherwise, etc. that further contribute to your uniqueness.

It might be good to think about your defined Better again. How we pursue our Better is who we are. No more banners, no more divisiveness unless we insist on living in Worse as a result of vagueness and stereotypes. If you want to know who we are, we are simply people who choose to pursue our own Better honorably. Nice to meet you.

¤ ¤ ¤

Inspired Right.

Defining Right

When we don't understand, what happens around us in life or our circumstances are not enjoyable. When we are not sure why things are the way they are, we are going to live in turmoil. Ever since our brains first supported critical thinking and curiosity, without achieving understanding there will be disorder and anxiousness inside of us. Disruption and disorder in our thinking, our decisions, our actions, and the outcomes.

For centuries thinkers, magicians, conmen, and crackpots have been trying to define the meaning of our lives, what is right for us, and then us building cultures around a limited, self-serving, or hidden agenda-based idea. We are no closer to "Better" and we should stop acting as if it is possible when we know deep down that it is not. No one defines Right but you. Our parents may keep us from hurting ourselves when we are young, and that is right.

But defining what we desire and what our life path should be is our responsibility alone. There is one original design of our sense of Right and it comes included in our welcome package at birth. Is there any point in trying to disprove or argue away our given sense of Right?

Group or mob rule expects us to concede our authority of individual Right. Dispelling individual Right makes sense only if you want to waste the time you have in your life for joy or to purposely take advantage of others.

The debate and the challenge of defining who we are is similar in complexity and futility as a one-size-fits-all meaning or purpose in life without including individual Right. The tough questions about defining who we are can be asked to stir the pot of bias or bigotry or they can be asked in search of real answers in a pursuit of our Better.

¤ ¤ ¤

Life Selfish

When we did our first draft of this book the subtitle was "Aiming for Life Selfish". Selfish freaked people out. Boy, did that go badly! Our work brought us to the conclusion that the only way to become inspired by Right and to break our addictions to Wrong was to become more selfish about the Better of our own lives in an honorable way.

Another of our discoveries, and a key one, is that selfish has a bad rap and is used against us as an obstacle in our path to Better. We also now see that personally selfish is not accurate in its use to describe our behavior in a super-consumer society. When we selfishly seek the people, jobs, possessions that are not right for us or able to satisfy us honorably, when honest, who's the selfish one? More so, what about the one that is encouraging us to pursue what is better for them?

If I am selfish about the big house instead of the small house and it is unfulfilling when I move in, who's selfishness have I satisfied? Probably the seller who over-priced it. If I step on others to increase my pay and appear selfish in my pursuit of promotion, while remaining unfulfilled and even more dissatisfied when I start the new work. Who's selfish am I satisfying?

Probably someone else who can benefit the most financially from my mercenary selfishness.

Selfish behavior is also included in our welcome package to life along with our sense of Right and desire for Better which means that there is goodness in selfish somewhere. Without selfish we would not aggressively prioritize eating. Without selfish we would not insist on breathing and fight when drowning. Without selfish there would be no such thing as "my life". Without selfish we would not strive to stand up. Everything we do includes selfish.

Selfish is a case of mistaken identity in our culture. Seriously, we have selfish as wrong as Right. Think about everything that you commit to regularly or that consumes big chunks of your life. Is it a selfish pursuit of your Better, or more likely to satisfy the Better of others? Even people you will never know or meet?

Now, this can seem complicated or even abstract, and we are about simple, so the point is you are not wrongly selfish if you are pursuing something Better for you with all you have in you. To selfishly avoid using the tactics of Wrong or selfishly and feverishly work to escape Worse is Right selfish. There. We called you selfish, life selfish. And we're darn glad we can if you step off and start to more purposely use your Right to get there.

Inspired Right.

Better Is Right

We wanted to get back to your first Compass Point. "Is Better right for you?". When given a multiple-choice question, we try to choose the better answer. Multiple choice suggests that we might not know the right answer completely, but we know enough to make the right choice. Sometimes we know the better answer, sometimes we guess.

Here's one, "Do you know the difference between Right and Wrong?". Multiple choice. Did you answer yes or no to knowing the difference? Was it a guess? We bet that you did not even hesitate with your answer. Of course, we know the difference, right? Knowing the difference between right and wrong for ourselves is universal common ground. This means we all share the knowledge and agree that it is true. Right is better than wrong. Which side would you pick in an argument regarding the better of the two?

Those who say that they do not know the difference are a significant minority or purposely dishonest or just don't care about life anymore if ever. Answering no might also suggest that you should take extra time with this book.

This is one of the easiest multiple choice questions of all time because we have the answer no matter where we went to school or how attentive our parents were to our development.

Knowing the difference between right and wrong arrives at simply the better answer. With Right being obviously better than Wrong when asked, why do we choose Right less than Wrong in our lives? We think it is because we do not use Right as a tool.

Because Right is better, it is the best foundational compass available to guide us. It will guide us all to only one place. It guides us to where or what is right or better for all of us. That is, if we are honest with ourselves about how we prioritize Better and we want to be first.

¤ ¤ ¤

Inspired Right.

Who Defines You?

Part Three

Obstructing Better

Root Cause

What stands in the way of our Better is the root cause of our anxiousness, fears, and pervasive dissatisfaction. Some of these obstacles are placed there by our own misunderstanding about our authority over our own sense of Right and our reliance on Wrong.

The outcomes, or the condition of Worse, is often a self-inflicted wound. Building a foundation guided by our sense of Right will address much of this negative phenomenon. More on that later.

Root cause is a term for the very core element(s) below all the stuff we see as bad or annoying in our lives. Like the root of a tree. Deep below the surface. With defying wonder roots go deeper and deeper or wider and wider in search of nutrients and Better. It is bound by what the environment offers.

If the environment is wrong for a tree and it only can find walls that limit its roots or pollution that poisons its being, the tree can look okay for a while above ground to the casual observer, but it will die a slow and what we can only assume to be a painful death.

Right is a root-worthy nutrient for humans, the universal, intelligent race.

Inspired Right.

When feeding our thinking, decisions, and actions with the direction of Right, our roots will see an endless growth path until the end of our natural lives. At the same time, getting to the root causes of our suspected or known Worse can sometimes take some digging.

We don't have to dig too far, just have a willingness to dig. The number one pollutant to our system that obstructs our Better is a reliance on the over-availability of the tactics of Wrong and the shaky, shifty, untrustworthy foundations we try to wrap our roots around. There are common obstructions that we'll talk about that stand between us and Better, but none more poisonous than the root cause of Wrong.

¤ ¤ ¤

Wrongaholism

Devastating addictions are awful. You know, those addictions that turn people into the walking dead. Strung out, nervous, disengaged, agitated about finding the next fix. Something that takes control of us, overpowers us, is relentless, is never satisfied or truly satisfying. Addictions are like trying to fill a bucket that has no bottom. The more you pour into it has no bearing on reaching the satisfaction of filling it.

It doesn't matter how much we steal, cheat, lie, hurt ourselves or others to try to fill that bucket of illusionary satisfactions, it will never be enough because the bucket is unfillable. Some know this to be true once in an addiction, but can't seem to help themselves to stop these futile acts without some trustworthy help. Many others just don't know when they are addicts. Particularly when we are addicted to the tactics of Wrong.

Ever know of a functioning alcoholic, or functioning drug, gambling, or pornography addict? You probably have an idea of what they are all about. These are the people who put on a great game face. You know, everything is cool on the outside. They have jobs, homes, families, responsibilities. And unless they screw up majorly you have no idea what's going on under the surface.

Underneath, their only priority is to get sauced, stoned or stimulated. Drink stuff that doesn't smell too bad, chew a lot of gum, self-medicate in a way that is not obvious and seems easy to hide, sneak time on phones or computers when no one can ever know that your brain is now craving images the same way heroin takes control. It does not take much exposure to then have our roots craving pollution.

From what we've learned, functioning addicts all have one thing in common. At least most of the functioning or undercover addicts believe that they are in control or that they don't have an addiction at all. There is a level of arrogance and overconfidence that they can put it down or stop anytime they want.

A little stimulation is what makes them feel alive. A little stimulation doesn't hurt anyone. In reality, the sense of not getting caught can become as exciting and motivating as the stimulant.

They also have something else in common. An undercurrent of fear. A nonstop pressure that steals any and all semblance of personal peace. And they never get to Better no matter how hard they try to use momentary stimulation to get there.

Feels like they almost touch Better for a moment, for a second, for a sensation. Then it's gone. It's faster than they are. So, the chase picks up again. Remember the bottomless bucket? Unfillable. Addicts rationalize that

Better somehow can become real through Wrong.

An addiction to Wrong might be small, might be big. Someone sees your Wrong in the open will define you by it. Are you someone in pursuit of Better, or you are a cheater, a liar, untrustworthy, unreliable, a fraud? Or are you arrogant and okay with life all wrong? You know, a captain of industry. "Who are they to judge me?", "I'm just human, I'm expected to do Wrong."

Like any addiction, we need something that is reliable and trustworthy to help us stop our ways and to change our behavior because it is better for us. The motivation to move away from Wrong must satisfy the same selfish energy we commit to hopeless pursuits.

Something that can help us stay out of the ditch in the future. Something we can use to warn our kids. Something that is better for us individually. Right is that something. But until we understood that our addiction to Wrong was Worse for us first and foremost, and not for others, we were stuck. We had to get selfish about Right.

¤ ¤ ¤

Inspired Right.

Powerless Person

Another obstacle in the way of our Better is our sense of individual weakness. There is an illusion that we can only find safety in numbers. We tend to group today because there is a sense that as an individual we lack the horsepower to blaze our own trails to Better. Thinking that it is no longer possible for one person to swim successfully against the tide of Wrong is not correct.

Those who promote wrong, represent wrong, enjoy wrong, those who fear "different" despite demanding that others honor them as different, whether individuals or groups, mostly fear the individual who thinks on their own. Relying on your Right is thinking for yourself.

It gives you everything that you need to define your Better and to pursue it with confidence. At every step of our journey we simply asked ourselves, "Is this right for me?" and "Is this better for me"? If no is the answer to either of these questions we navigated away or worked our way out more powerfully.

To think that we are individually powerless against our time within a negatively dominant Today, and that others are better at thinking for us as a path of least resistance, is where we end up without relying on the help of our Compass.

Without it, many of us are virtually defenseless. With it, we can debunk Wrong consistently and stand on our own. We have full power to move in a new direction right now by stopping the habit of hurting ourselves via ignoring our sense of Right. Self-inflicted wounds are our decisions that can stop us from achieving a fulfilled life.

Wounds and behavior that prevent us from being the people, the vibrant communities and the amazing country that most of us suspect we have the resources and the capabilities to become if not again, for the first time.

One Better at a time is so much more powerful than a regrettably dissatisfying group.

¤ ¤ ¤

Inspired Right.

Vaguely Better

The next obstacle in the way of our Better is vagueness. It is time to stop being fuzzy about Better if we want it. That was an early observation for us. If Better is a generalized goal or objective chances are we will fail to get there. Anyone who ever succeeded at anything knows that goals and objectives without clear definition are destined to fail. Expect to fail in your pursuit of Better if you do not wring out vague.

Looking closer at both group and individual Betters we found blatant vague. Group Better is when more than one person is expected to want the same Better. Remember the billions of combinations that contribute to our individuality? Group Better is undefinable. Individual is your own Better. In each case, the lack of definition is a key, yet a correctable flaw in the pursuit of Better.

"Let's make our community better." This group Better is not well defined or actionable. Any surprise that these initiatives regularly fizzle out or fail? Replace community with country, company, school, etc., and we see widespread vague. "Better" is well intentioned but highly unlikely without the buy-in of everyone. There must be something in it for everyone.

"I want a better life." Can anyone take specific action on this one? Replace life with relationship, marriage, job, etc., and we start to see the problem with our vagueness. Better for you can become more than a feel-good sentence, a romantic idea, or a personal whim by simply, honestly defining your Better on purpose and paying attention to it regularly. Our opportunity for Better success goes way up when it is defined, and we'd guess that there is nothing vague about what you think is better or right for you in all areas of your life. Right now.

Defining your own Better should be easy for you, right? And it is when we use our Compass of Right to verify our choices. By the way, no one is ever allowed to define your Better for you. That's our rule. More on this ahead.

¤ ¤ ¤

Better Lottery

Can your sense of bad luck stand in your way of Better? Have you looked across the street, down the road, up the hill with envy? Do you suspect that someone else's life is better than yours? Do you think the void in your Better can be filled with things?

Maybe some people are just luckier than you. Maybe some won the Better family lottery and you didn't. Maybe some won the ethnic lottery, and you didn't. Maybe, just maybe, you have no idea how dissatisfied those you envy might be.

Until now you may not have spent much time on purpose defining what you want from life. You don't have to win a lottery for the chance to do so. Isn't it fascinating that some, including us, had envy, emptiness, and anxiousness about a better life and we had never defined it for ourselves?

How can we monitor our progress or adjust our course with Right if we don't define where we want to go? If we are going to get all frothy about how we are getting taken advantage of or left behind in the wake of others we should know what we think that they are keeping us from.

Define specifically what we want in our lives so we see any gaps to Better and close those gaps with the Compass of Right. We can also stop complaining once we take control of our authority to use our sense of Right.

No one is keeping Better from you but you, more than likely. One cool thing happened when we started to define our Better with purpose. A lot of our day was found to be Worse or Wrong for us and we were able to start picking things and people we needed to jettison from our life. Jettisoned from our minds.

Once we did that we found that there were fewer uncontrollable obstacles between our Better than we first thought. When our Better targets and goals changed, anything not directly supporting the pursuit of those targets was let go. All the stuff we let go made room for more of our Better. We are in control of our Better. There is not luck involved in having the opportunity to pursue Better. This is a choice we make daily and how you paint your Better is just for you.

Better is all yours. It doesn't match up with anyone else's. Your Better is rare, just like you, meaning that what you want as a foundation is truly valuable to you. Priceless, in fact.

Why go looking elsewhere to replace or discard an original, one-of-a-kind Better with an imitation or a counterfeit Better we think others may have? There is no logical reason to replace your Better at all. Your Better is perfect for you once you define it and go after it.

¤ ¤ ¤

Burden Of Proof

One of the most tiresome thoughts about establishing our own Better is the thought that we are going to have to defend it against all enemies foreign and domestic. We compare it to the burdens we already have proving to outsiders that we picked a good side that we know is not based on Right or that we are in the right group that has no clear definition of Better.

Our energies are committed to tirelessly defending our choices and disproving the position of others instead of pursuing or presenting a real opportunity of Better in a positive, respectful manner.

The phenomenon of digging heals in once we pick a side even if it is not a perfect side for us happens because we have compromised our Better either consciously or subconsciously and are now forced to defend it.

We see this in our behavior today when we "listen" to respond instead of "listening" to understand so that we can learn. We often know with our inner sense of Right that we are promoting something that is suspect in some or a lot of ways. Where we end up in all of this is Worse.

Worse for us will continue every time we distrust our Right and ignore its warnings to steer away from Wrong and the groups that promote it.

Inspired Right.

Defending Wrong and Worse is comparable to bailing out a sinking ship with a paper cup to keep it afloat. There is no way to stop the water from coming, so we bail faster and harder.

Defending Worse or Wrong is exhausting. No wonder our lives are seen more as burdensome than opportunity-filled. Here's some good news. Knowing your Better and relying on the Compass of Right to guide you takes away all the group or side-picking burdens of proof forever.

No more wearing ourselves out learning to master group rhetoric or plotting against the views or opinions of the enemy as a staple in our day. No more defense-oriented anxiousness and anger fatigue.

There is no burden in proving that you made the right choice by pursuing what is right or better for you. That's an easy conversation. Think of the surprise when you let others know that the side you picked is you.

No one can argue against your Better or convince you otherwise successfully unless you allow them to take advantage of you.

No one can argue against your definition of Better if they know what that is, or you help them to understand that they have a unique Better, too.

No Better is more valid than yours. With your expanding understanding and appreciation for your Better and your Compass of Right, the burden of proof falls on everyone else to defend their vagueness and shifting foundations. Defending your Better is like pressing the easy button.

¤ ¤ ¤

Everything In It For You

Do you think that Wrong can get you to Better? We believe and we act as if Wrong has everything in it that we need to get us to true satisfaction and our desires and that Right is a weak alternative. In our today, wrong certainly appears to have more in it for us selfishly than Right.

We are not sure when the rat race began formally, but our valuing of Wrong is certainly the foundation for a hyper-consumption, unfulfilling culture. Wrong as a custom promotes and accepts rat-like, vicious fighting for 'ours' and the fight for 'mine' with no holds barred in the ring. The rat race is not competed within the rules of individual Right. It is competed within the arena of buckets without bottoms.

At the risk of missing out completely on the thrill that may come from being a part of a rat infestation, we decided to play our game by the rules and within the spirit of Right because Wrong was not getting us to Better. We wanted to take the possibility of an alternative more seriously to find out if there was more in it for ourselves than we are led to believe.

To our pleasant surprise, we were not only able to test Right easily, we were able to find Right increasingly, selfishly more satisfying than Wrong. Doing all it takes to get what we want is justified. Particularly if it involves a life impacting topic.

Just like not standing idly by without oxygen, food, water. We do whatever it takes to survive in our honorable pursuit of Better. What about doing all it takes to get money or possessions regardless of ethics, morals, or fairness? Any regrets? If you know any regrets, you know the difference between Right and Wrong.

Interestingly, within our deeper investigation into Right we found that what we thought we wanted was not always better for us in the first place. Right could be used in more situations where we had relied solely or heavily on Wrong as our guidance resulting in us being destructive to ourselves or others as a part of "doing all it takes".

Ironically, we were hurting ourselves and others to get something we knew our sense of Right would reject. The wrong job, deeper debt for another purchase, multiple purchases of the same thing, giving our entire person to someone not committed to us, and other prizes in the rat race.

We must focus on the point of stopping the pursuit of that which is not valuable or fulfilling to us individually versus what is. To pursue anything without it being right for us or better for us is a waste of time, energy, and resources, particularly if we know that our pursuits are not getting us any closer to Better and we do it anyway.

Bad Different

Avoiding different is not just an obstacle it is a trap that will pierce the skin, break bone, and create infectious wounds on the path to Better if not avoided. Is being different something to avoid or the trap of likeness? Let's re-establish right now that we are all guaranteed to be different no matter how hard we try not to be. It is a for sure, an absolute, an unavoidable reality.

Remember the billions of combinations in our secret recipes? So how is it that being different is wrong if it is unavoidable? Are we going to stop ourselves from pursuing what is Better or Right for us because of the fear of not fitting into something not right for us and we know it? Different today means being forced to pick a side.

Each side has the extreme of either dropping off the radar to become invisible enough to avoid conflict or becoming an agitator or militant willingly for the side we chose. Militant likeness today is packaged and sold to wrongly promote bi-directional bigotry, racism, discrimination, and exclusion.

When asked, many militants are not totally sure what they are militant about. First, they haven't accurately defined themselves if they do not know their honorable Better. These militants are just confused and scared. They are sure that belonging to something is better than belonging to nothing.

How we abuse the fascinating reality of different today proves that we've completely lost sight of the value of applying the knowledge of Right and how to use it to our advantage. Extinguishing different is not right.

We have no one on the planet that is the same as anyone of us, right? So how is being angry about different right? Different has always represented a great opportunity for discovery. Different promotes the encouragement of curiosity. Different wakes up our pallet. We used to be wondrous about different.

What changed? Is different still out there? Are we all so self-aware and desensitized by information technology overload that different does not exist? We expect a lot of different answers and we are okay with that.

¤ ¤ ¤

Any Compass Will Work

Do you want to stay off the path to your Better or in the ditch? If you do, then continue to use and shuffle the multiple compasses that contradict your Right. There is an old expression that if you are too open minded your brains will fall out. Today, when it comes to choosing what guides us, our compasses if you will, there are more sources of guidance than areas to apply them. Keeping on a solid foundation or moving in a trustworthy direction is a guaranteed headache.

Many of the tactics of Wrong are thought to be compasses. Their use is common, acceptable, and promoted. Keep using them instead of Right and the farther away from your Better you will get. We have compasses for work, for school, for intimacy, for health, for finances, for faith, for non-faith, for parenting, for mentoring, for leading, for following, and on and on.

What if we had one that we could trust and one that would work well everywhere? We do. And we all, each one of us, has it. Right now. No kidding. It may be dormant, turned off, ignored, distrusted, devalued, or screaming at us, but we have it.

The rest of our compass options are like a flavor of the month. They'll change, they must as people involved change.

What this means is a great opportunity in our hands, right now, to debunk every single situation and obstacle standing in the way of our Better whether we put it there ourselves previously or not.

¤ ¤ ¤

Can You See Better?

Part Four

Compass of Right

The Right Ethic

Compasses are what guide us. Ethics is one compass we are familiar with. However, when we hear the word "ethics" used these days it is almost always associated with a story about someone or some organization that has violated them. Or ethics is a program that is structured around avoiding being accused of violating them. Organizations teach ethics for compliance with a mandate that good behavior be reinforced and paid attention to. Ethics programs inconsistently guide behavior.

The hope that people will stay on the straight and narrow line because of a class or mandate addressing ethical behavior is about as likely to happen as our community magically arriving at Better with our currently undefinable approach. A positive outcome from our current approach to ethics can only be a hope and never an expectation.

Ethics is one of many vague compasses that hold unreasonable expectations for successful guidance because of the multitude of definition variations possible or already in force. Ethics, like traditional interpretations of Right when applied to specific situations, or "situational Right", is an assumed obligation outside of written law. It can be associated with a "moral code", whatever that means.

Inspired Right.

These various types of Right can only be defined for a very specific or situational application and can be confusing.

However, one compass definition stands out clearly and consistently and that is our personal sense of Right. As a referenceable source of guidance, our Right is consistent without the need to review any laws, programs, mandates, or voted on definition. Ethics and the various situational Right compass have little or no success because there is limited to no buy in from people not seeing enough in it for themselves.

What if ethical behavior was provable to have a direct connection to Better? What if our moral code were specific to the satisfaction of the individual based on their own sense of Right? What if being honorable was beneficial to the individual first, having something selfishly within it for them? How can that be taught? How can that be enforced? How can non-compliance be punished? Could we elevate good outcomes from hope to highly probable? What if the Compass of Right could replace ethics programs and deliver the results we hope for?

The right ethic is the one that is determined by a personal sense of what is Right and what points to an individual, honorable pursuit of Better. For those who subscribe to the personal Right philosophy there will be less pain and more joy.

Personal satisfaction, gratitude and appreciation for honoring oneself, avoiding regrets, arriving at and staying within our individual right to peace of mind and contentment. "You mean to say that if I don't steal there is more in that for me than if I did?" Yes, but only if your Better is defined.

When we know for sure or are reasonably certain that our decisions and actions will keep us on our path to joy or knock us off, which are we most likely to choose?

What law or mandate will I need to ensure I stay on my own path? It is our internal, personal, given sense of Right that turned into ethics and moral code definitions when someone decided that their Right should be the standard and everyone else's should comply.

And if you were not willing to be in line with my Right, which can only point to my Better, then you should be punished. General ethics and moral codes were berthed within a selfish, dishonorable pursuit of a particular agenda that someone disguised as Better.

The proper activation of our Compass of Right is what is needed to steer us personally and collectively away from hope and into Better reality.

¤ ¤ ¤

Painful Right

Have you ever noticed that doing right is thought to be something painful or sacrificial? That Right is facing outward and not inward? If we are not experiencing enough pain from "doing the right thing" we probably are not doing it right or enough. If you haven't figured this out, sacrificial Right is not motivational and it is not often well received. That's why more people aren't doing it more often.

They don't see what's in it for them other than satisfying their annual Right quota. If we don't do enough for others, put others perceived to be less fortunate than ourselves before ourselves, someone will use the tactic of guilt to try and goad us into action. How painful is it to suffer through guilt-laden sessions of serving turkey once a year to homeless people? Most of us will begrudgingly commit to some form of "doing the right thing" and end up feeling used or guilty for not doing more. Unfortunately, "doing the right thing" becomes a quota and not an inspirational way of live.

Being psychologically forced to do right is painful and being on the receiving end of unsolicited advances in the name of Better are too. Ever been on the receiving end of someone "doing the right thing" and it is not better for you at all?

This happens a lot once people pick a side. People drink some flavor of Better that overwhelms and stupefies them and then come wholesale into their day with a commitment to espouse their Better on all passersby.

Presumptuous and arrogant on their part. Not well received on our part. What if doing the right thing for yourself was selfishly satisfying to you first and those around you became better or happier because of it? Would you do it more?

Would Better become overwhelmingly popular if it was not chained to the concept of "doing the right thing" for others? Would personal Better on a broad scale retire so much Worse and Wrong that doing the right thing for others would become less and less necessary, even obsolete?

We believe just about everyone has a heart to help and to give. Examples of the purist generosity we've ever witnessed came from those with little or less materially than most. At the same time, some of the best or biggest potential givers to the support of community Better don't give because of the untrustworthy, agenda-full Better of the asker.

Better could prevail without any pain if we commit to a personal sense of Right as our primary, trustworthy source of guidance.

The outcomes of a Right-based pursuit of Better in life would eliminate the need to drag others into our own addiction to Wrong and condition of Worse. Our own Better means we are less of a burden on others, which is simply better for everyone.

¤ ¤ ¤

Confused Right

Without defining our Better, the destinations in life best for us, where we are and where we are going can be confusing. Life can become a series of dead ends or seem to just move in circular motions where we get nowhere. A compass we can trust is the only way to pick the best destinations and to help us along the way as we work to get there.

Our sense of Right, our Compass of Right, and its guidance capabilities from day ones only direct us strongly to Better and away from Worse. Then why are we so confused about using Right?

The guilt trip version of Right can confuse us because it is not always clear whose Better we are satisfying. There are plenty of people or forces in the world that can also confuse us about Right because they are not interested in promoting our supporting our own pursuit of Better.

Maybe there are other reasons that might make sense as to why we don't enthusiastically jump on our own Right train. But others are not why we don't rely on our sense of Right proudly and unapologetically. It appears to us that Right is not used as the guidance tool within the capacity of its original design because we think we are smart enough all on our own and don't need its help.

Inspired Right

Wouldn't it be awesome if we had a tool so we didn't have to make mistakes to learn? So we wouldn't have to look to the past to be able to enable a successful future? We all have this tool in our Compass of Right.

We certainly are not confused about knowing the difference between Right and Wrong for ourselves, and are well familiar with the condition of Worse, but our arrogance tells us that we can easily learn from our mistakes and recover from our mistakes as wisdom that can best guide us instead of dodging Worse all along.

Sure, we can be aware of some mysterious tugging in our bellies in times of uncertainty or confusion but that little thing cannot be stronger than our ego or our raw will to crash and burn as a learning experience, right? Well, wrong.

Our inner sense of Right is a level of knowledge that correctly anticipates the impact of what a bad move towards newness or a misdirected action while in the middle of confusion can do to our Better. Our sense of Right is so strong that it will tell us the correct course well before we physically or personally experience Wrong for a reason.

Right is a highly-sophisticated warning and directional system within every connected cell of our body that uses our sight, smell, taste, touch and emotions to our mind telling us very clearly to beware or to move ahead.

Our sense of Right is who we are. It cannot be surgically removed, it cannot be cosmetically improved, but it can be stupidly ignored.

When we ignore it is when we become the most confused about our direction in life. There is no confusion about the outcomes ahead if we go in a bad direction on purpose while ignoring our compass.

¤ ¤ ¤

Compass Essentials

When pilots take the responsibility of a flight from one city to another they apply the training, experience, and the tools at their disposal to arrive when expected and where expected. They are successful often without ever being in a destination city before. A compass is essential for success.

Pilots utilize compass technology that has advanced and become highly precise compared to other or earlier compasses. The compass can eliminate journey error, anxiousness, eliminate the need for extra effort, prevent wasting resources, and make the journey fun and satisfying. Without it, all bets for the best possible journey are off.

On any given trip, the course is corrected and adjusted, many if not thousands of times as temperature, wind, airspeed, atmospheric pressure, weather, mechanical issues and other factors can work to push a plane and the pilot off course. Without a reliable, trustworthy compass, a one-degree move off course could have the pilot, crew, and passengers far off course, off course forever, or even bracing for impact. "Brace for impact!", is not the announcement we want to hear in our journeys.

Our sense of Right as our compass makes this announcement a lot on our journey in life even if we don't listen to it. Why have the most advanced compass ever made at the ready twenty-four seven and ignore it? This compass is amazing. It never needs upgrades. It never needs maintenance. It doesn't have parts that break. It doesn't require years of training to master, and it is not corruptible by weather, wind speed, disasters or the actions of others.

Can you see the rest of your life ahead unfolding without anything new or unpredictable happening? Unless locked in solitary somewhere, most of us will have uncharted stuff ahead of us personally, professionally and in our communities. Unpredictable journeys have good outcomes only when we use a compass that we can trust. We want to stay on course.

We want journeys without friction, errors and self-inflicted wounds. The compass we choose to rely on dictates all of this. Looking back into our lives for a moment, were there any incidents or circumstances that you wish you had better guidance before getting into trouble or a sticky situation? Your Compass of Right is that guidance moving forward.

¤ ¤ ¤

Inspired Right.

True Right

We want to trust what guides us and that the direction is "true". This means that the direction is accurate and trustworthy. True, truth, and trust are all dependent on the availability of a universal Right. Our sense of Right will not purposely direct us to use Wrong or to arrive at Worse. Wrong is a tactic we learn, Worse is where we end up if we don't pay attention to our sense of Right. True?

This means that our sense of Right, something we all have, is a truth. It cannot be denied that it exists universally. It cannot be proven to be untrustworthy, and we trust that it always has our best interests in mind.

Other than our own sense of Right, where else can you find guidance that can stand up to the tests of true, truth, and trust? A reliance on our own compass can be scary to ourselves at first and a threat to others over time. When we know more about our Right and we prove to ourselves that it has more in it for us than Wrong we can become comfortable and confident that Right can be applied to conversations and actions to fully push Wrong and Worse off of our paths.

"Is what you are telling me true?", "How do I know if you are telling the truth?", "How can I trust you to do what is right?" are all questions that we ask openly or silently because we are interested in what is right or better for us personally when interacting with others.

If others are not guided by a sense of Right and on the path to an honorable pursuit of Better, you can never know for sure. How would we find out? It's called conversation. Try it with a little Right for a change.

Do we hold or are we prepared to hold ourselves to the same level of standards for true, truth, and trust? If you recall, one of the keys to a successful journey to Better is personal honesty. We can honestly hold ourselves to the same high standard of true if we purposely decide that Better is right for us and Worse is not and mean it. Then standards become easy.

Our sense of Right is our standard. We already have it in us. Better for us and us becoming better for others is possible and real once we rely on and prioritize the guidance of our given, indisputable sense of Right.

¤ ¤ ¤

Inspired Right.

Proving Right

We love the idea that we need proof of something before we will buy in. We don't always have to have personal proof before we decide. Lots of times we take the word of others that something is proved to be or do what is advertised and that it will improve our condition.

We want stuff, new stuff, different stuff. Or we want to be included, to join, to keep up with others. But we want proof, or the illusion of proof, first.

So, we listen to or read about the opinions and experiences of spokespeople, celebrities, customer reviews, polls, surveys, and more as a part of our "prove it to me first" process of buying or buying in. Somebody's always selling us something even if we aren't shopping. The believe that they've already proved on our behalf that it is a good thing for us. Very nice of them.

Have you ever been disappointed after buying something or buying into a group or philosophy despite the high recommendations or ratings of others? The risk of relying on others as a vote of confidence to move ahead with anything is that they have no way of communicating exactly how the product, service, or event is going to impact your Better one way or the other.

They don't know your Better but assume that you want to be just like them.

Do we need proof that our sense of Right is better for us before we commit to using it regularly? Do we need a study, some data, a workgroup session, some opinions because we don't want to be the first to try this new thing or idea? How do we know this Compass of Right will work? We are having a little fun here. You already know it works. It's been talking to your senses forever.

The real question is if you need proof that Better is what you want. Just like your definition of Better, wanting it is your decision. We all have proved to ourselves that the tactics of Wrong are not a guidance system we can trust and it never has Better as the ultimate objective.

We will continue to prove to ourselves that our unwillingness to follow our own sense of Right in what we think, decide, and act will result in Worse. Worse is less fulfilling than Better and is not hard to prove.

The opportunity you have ahead is to see for yourself that it takes larger amounts of energy, time, and commitment to arrive at Worse and master Wrong that to use your sense of Right to your personal advantage.

¤ ¤ ¤

Inspired Right.

Honestly Right

Are you fatigued by conversations in our day constantly calling out our need to be honest or the expectation that others be more honest? How about completely honest? Is that possible? The topic of honesty can pin us down, expose our warts, make us feel guilty, find us to be guilty.

Honesty, being honorable, doing the right thing, are all for those do-gooders who have no idea how much fun it is to live in Worse. Thank goodness that they are the minority today.

We give each other the get-out-of-honesty card for liberal use with the thinking, "I'm only human. No one is perfect. Forgive me.", instead of admitting that we have no true direction and a weak commitment to the joy of being alive.

This cultural and widespread habit of dodging or rationalizing away honesty can become a source of humor and irony when we begin to use our Compass of Right on purpose. Our inner sense of what is right for us or better for us gives us the chance to be perfectly honest always and laugh about it, have joy within it.

Honestly, what we think, decide, and do is either better or worse for us personally. Can you be honest about what is better for you? Then be honest and act on it.

You now know a simple person's definition of the meaning of life. Life means that you must make a choice between Better or Worse and be honest about your choice. (Apologies to all the complicated philosophers out there. Keep up the good work.)

Life means you are keenly alive in a pursuit of Better or walking dead mired in Worse. Alive is the idea behind our human existence. Had you ever thought how simple life was designed to be and how simple it can really become when always guided by Right?

We had been overcomplicating so much of our lives by getting onto paths that do not lead to Better. We brought so much anxiety and dissatisfaction on to ourselves by not being honest about defining our Better.

And we were lying to ourselves and others when not honest about wanting Better bad enough to completely deny Wrong and Worse. Activating our sense of personal Right changes all that.

¤ ¤ ¤

Inspired Right.

See Better Ahead

The right compass can direct you to your Better and help you to see through the clouds of Worse blocking your view to a better path. It can direct you around the piles of the wrong junk littering and obstructing your path. It can navigate through and around the wall of people in your way who have no interest in Better. Your Compass of Right sees beyond all of this. You must begin to trust it to see for yourself until all the obstructions are behind you.

Trusting the Compass of Right is the same as trusting your ability to know the difference between what is right or wrong for you. We talk later about establishing your own Foundation for Better and this is what you will stand on to see above and beyond the garbage in your way today.

The beauty of being able to have your compass see for you until you see it better yourself is that it will keep pulling your mind's eye in the direction you prefer to go without you having to have all the answers, solutions, or definitions to a better life in advance of starting to move.

What is in front of our eyes is what we pay attention to and if it is Worse we can get stuck there without seeing Better ahead. We move to where our eyes focus. Focusing on the simple directional pull of the compass can draw our eyes, or mind's eye, away from Worse and away from our reliance on the tactics of Wrong.

You have heard that a body in motion tends to stay in motion. You cannot move in two separate directions at the same time. Once your thoughts, decisions, and actions are guided to your Better or the general direction of Better Worse and Wrong will move out of your view.

The key to beginning to move ahead with more purpose and confidence towards your Better is to recognize the junk on your path for what it is. Be honest and call all junk, all naysayers, all predators, all dissatisfaction Worse for you.

Start to stop others from taking the liberty of putting junk in your way. Junk that will pull your eyes and attention away from your visibility to Better. Start to say no to junk as fast as you used to say yes to junk or let junk clutter your path.

¤ ¤ ¤

Better Inside

The Compass of Right can tell you if your destinations are truly right or better for you. It can also show the best route to get there. It can also tell you when you have arrived at Better. You know this sensation as contentment, fulfilment, and peace of mind. You feel better inside.

We arrive at Better in the major aspects of our lives the same way as we arrive at Better in the incremental or incidental destinations of Better but they are prioritized differently.

In relationships, the right or better person for each of us should be more purposely discovered and cultivated. If we find the idea of togetherness and journeying together to be better than a life alone this element of Better is a major aspect of our lives.

If a new car that won't die on the freeway is a destination or element of Better this is an incremental or incidental Better. It gives us mental rest and comfort. Stimulating our taste buds with pizza or caviar may be better than canned beans, but stimulation is seldom sustainable or a destination or element of our Better.

It can make our journey more fun, but we can be at our Better or pursuing our Better without it, too. Although the elements of what may define our individual Betters are unique to us, the outcome of joy or knowing we've arrived at Better as an emotion or sensation that is the same for everyone. There is nothing better, if you will.

The idea or the memory of the experience of fulfillment, contentment, and peace of mind is what motivates us to move ahead and work to find what satisfies us the most.

The difference between true joy and dishonorable satisfaction, although confused by many to be the same sensation, is that dishonorable satisfaction is achieved by using the tactics of Wrong and taking advantage of someone else in a bad or disrespectful way.

We cannot decide for you what will bring you the most joy. We cannot say with any real definition what it will or does take for each of us to get to Better and to stay there.

We can say, however, that mercenary pursuits of incremental or incidental Better cannot compare to the satisfaction and joy of achieving a Better defined by each of us individually and pursued honorably.

Better is the oasis of success found by those who put their Right first.

¤ ¤ ¤

Keen Eye For The Obvious

Our conscience, our "gut-feel", our inner sense of Right may not have been known to us as our Compass of Right before now. You may label it some other way that helps you to use it more regularly. We like the phrase because it describes the functionality of Right as a tool we all need as well as the availability of its powerful truth.

We did not invent Better and we certainly did not invent our sense of Right. We just needed a keen eye to see the obvious value of Right within the layers of Wrong and the wet blanket of Worse that dominates our days. We all have the same keen eye capable of seeing our Better if we want to use it.

The obvious or most straight forward way to Better may take some peeling back of Worse but Better dominates the horizons for anyone interested in being fully alive and looking ahead with interest. Worse blocks us from seeing any meaningful horizon so we need to start jettisoning the junk off our path and out of our line of sight.

We want to encourage everyone to know that Better is in front of all of us and sticking with Right can help us break our addition to Wrong simply by adjusting our targets and moving our attentions in a direction that we know is best for us.

This change in our behavior is easy and can start right now. The more we use Right to guide us the more obvious our opportunities for Better can become. Better is all around us, we just need to use the same keen eye that we use to focus on Worse and to now seek out Better.

¤ ¤ ¤

Do You Know Your Right?

Part Five

Right In Common

What Anyone Wants

Better is what anyone wants, or should want if they see their life as a gift of opportunity and exploration of the new and different. This is a very general idea that, as we've learned, does not become actionable or interesting until some definition is provided.

Our own Better needs to be clearly defined and adjusted as we go through different seasons in life if we want to move ahead with any sense of accomplishment and progress. Our group our community Better could improve greatly if there was even the most basic of accommodation by our leaders for the genuine, honorable interests of each of us as we define them.

So, when we say that Better is what anyone wants it includes the condition that we are not able to pursue joy or achieve honorable Better by ourselves like when stranded alone on a desert island.

Knowing some of the people we know and working in some of the conditions we work in may make the thought of an island attractive, but that intimacy thing and that sense of shared joy thing we desire will escape us for sure.

Ultimately, what anyone wants is their own Better to be in motion while the Betters of others are in motion at the same time.

Inspired Right.

This creates the energy and the positive sense that life is good both personally and collectively. This may sound a little socialistic, utopian, unoriginal, or naïve, but our own pursuits of Better are anything but a social program or communal obligation in disguise.

Our own Better includes establishing companies, creating jobs, teaching our children to think for themselves and understand the pursuit of Better, creating art to be shared and to be compensated along the way, leading with lasting impact, finding that beach house or high rise or ranch, improving science, improving health, and on and on. Better is endless and it is often seen in the tangible as well as within us. Better mousetraps are good!

Each of these individual Betters require contributions from others and infinite numbers of interactions with others by every person who crosses main street socially or professionally.

Main street today is digital or physical. In each case, we have opportunities to take our eyes off Worse and redirect them to a defined Better that we can all get excited about because it has something in it for all of us.
Exclusion and division survives and thrives only when we are not honest about a pursuit of Better.

To personally pursue our Better, we must understand and recognize how to utilize what we all have in common. Despite our uniqueness, every human has a lot in common with every other human. Also, Better does not have to include arm twisting, angry circular debate, or fear of loss when we exercise a keen eye for our similarities.

The more we recognize and agree on our similarities, or what we have in common, we do not have to sacrifice our uniqueness. Identical sameness does not work in the pursuit of Better. Commonality does.

¤ ¤ ¤

Fascinating Right

Our group may fascinate easily, but the more we thought about, discussed, and applied the guidance of Right to all aspects of our lives the outcomes ranged from basic cool all the way to stunningly awesome. This opportunity is something that we all have in common.

To put it into motion each of us simply decides that we want Better in a new way or for the first time and that Right is a viable tool to try in succeeding differently than we had in the past.

Some of the fascinating outcomes included the discovery of all the places where Right fits. Not only where it fits but how the need for multiple sources of guidance can go away and take with them the confusion and apathy they create. Using our sense of Right first fits in our thinking. Right only points to Better so we begin to only concentrate and focus on Better.

We became more optimistic about jettisoning Wrong and the weight of Worse from our minds by simply evaluating if what consumed our thoughts was intended or capable of getting us to Better or supporting the fears of failure and being left out or behind. Where we looking ahead or over our shoulders?

We found that Right fits perfectly into the process of making all our decisions. We could become more honest and comfortable with our decisions because we had a standard of truth to compare all the options to. That truth being the voice or force of our sense of Right that we knew we could trust in all situations. If a decision was going to knock us off the path to our Better or keep us there in any aspect of our life, we found it really easy to choose.

It is fascinating how simple thinking and decisions can become when we are not obligated to include the desires of others as the primary objective in our lives. Remember, life selfish is not mercenary. The real fascination happens when we act or take actions based on the guidance of Right. This is what others will see or experience resulting from our new thinking and our decisions.

If they have come to expect our actions to be less than honorable or wicked this change for the better for ourselves can knock them off their feet as they see it unfold. It may also take a while for others to trust that you are not hiding something up your sleeve or that you are not trying to dupe them with your kindness and a stabbing motion is soon to follow. If they see you coming out of poor health or financial slavery because you decide that neither of these is part of your Better, it can deliver equally fun reactions.

Keep in mind that you pursue Better for you. Can you start to see how it is also better for others?

Inspired Right.

Positive change, particularly when it is so tangible for ourselves personally is the fascinating opportunity that we have in front of and within us all.

What fascinates us when it comes to applying Right will ultimately begin to inspire us to seek Better more. The opportunity to become inspired by Right is something that we all also have in common.

¤ ¤ ¤

Better Is Right

This revelation is another point of reference for our commonality. We've used this statement a few times already but this point is important to pay attention to. If we think that others should respect our individual pursuits of Better, then we must reciprocate. Better is Right and Worse is Wrong is an easy point of reference and topic of conversation that is undeniably true, and capable as an initial or lasting source of agreement.

By focusing in on our own Better and activating with purpose our sense of Right we are going to recognize the same behavior in others when it happens. There will be no need to attack their Better or be afraid of their Better if it is honorable. If it is not honorable and it is being forced on us, another commonality is to defend ourselves and our path to Better with our Compass of Right.

We all have the opportunity and the ability to fend off the wicked and move away from Wrong and Worse if we listen to or pay attention to our compass and follow its directions.

If we know that Better is undeniably right for all of us individually, then we also know that we hold a minority positon in our culture.

Those addicted to Wrong and ensnared by Worse outnumber the Better faithful today by a wide margin. We once had this addiction and living condition in common so we understand it. Our dissatisfaction with it drove us to finding a way to become inspired and motivated differently.

As people, once we find freedom or crack some secret code about life we want to get on our soapbox and preach. Enthusiasm about Better whether real or otherwise can have us thinking, "You don't know what you are missing. You must start to think and live like me!". Another thing we have in common is that we find those who can't carry themselves with restraint and respect are found to be annoying and worthy of our anger.

Our fascination, shock and joy, and renewed interest in a realistic pursuit of Better has us at some of the highest levels of enthusiasm ever experienced in our adult lives. Recovering and finding our way back after losing or having the sense of joy that can only come from Right taken from us could easily put us on a soapbox. We're excited.

But our compass tells us that boasting goes against our sense of Right and could obstruct our pursuit of Better.

¤ ¤ ¤

The Right Origin

Life starts right if we are born. A burdened or unsatisfactory life may encourage us to forget this. Our knowledge of our own sense of Right is with us in that welcome package on day one along with a selfish desire to be alive, among other cool things. We can learn or are forced to learn the definitions of Right created by people or groups over time but the original sense of Right is not activated, energized, shaped, or influenced by worldly definitions.

Our sense of Right insists on a pursuit of Better advantageous to each of us if we allow it to guide us. Our parents, our siblings, our neighbors may have worldly and original Right all wrong and are not reliable or capable enough to give it to us properly, consistently, or honorably.

This is why our original, given sense of Right is so valuable. It is the only source of guidance that will not change with the seasons, the economy, the geography, or the culture. In any time and any environment, it only points us towards our Better or our way out of Worse.

This is true for all of us. Original Right is something we all have in common and provable if we are breathing and our minds are functional enough to use it. The composition of our welcome package to life is not up to us.

Inspired Right.

Yet we are given all that we need to grow and go in good ways given the opportunity.

The use of the word "miracle" is common in conversations about birth and life. Some miracles can be explained to the acceptance of many and some cannot.

Life and birth are miracles or sources of wonderment only if we take advantage of what we are given. There is nothing miraculous about taking the first and last breath with nothing but Wrong and Worse in between.

Wonderment can persist with Wrong and Worse but only if we are scratching our heads trying to figure out how Wrong or Worse could possibly be a viable substitute for our Better.

¤ ¤ ¤

Common Ground

We prefer to be with people that have something in common with us. What if everyone had something in common? Would we be more excited about being around people, all people, regardless of skin tone, economics, gender or life-style preferences if our interactions could support or promote our Better without bias or agenda? We have plenty in common, yet the excitement about positively interacting with anyone crossing our path is missing. Why is that?

First, we feel that not enough people are truly focused on honorable Better. When we are not, the differences of others overpower our commonality because we think we have to either learn and be assimilated or perish. Let's just call it fear out of our mutual ignorance regarding Right.

This fear of the assumed unconditional terms of assimilation, one group out numbering another group, hurts us all. It is not better for anyone. Not better for those outsiders that fear the group and not right for those in the group driving an agenda that does not line up with their individual Better.

If we are going to have freer space to pursue our own Better, we will need to openly and formally address our commonality and come to agreement that each of us has the right to the same opportunity in an honorable pursuit of Better without being militant or dishonest.

This agreement does not include conceding anything that contributes to our own Better or what our sense of Right tells us is ours.

¤ ¤ ¤

Obviously In Common

Let's list a few things to consider that we all have in common and things that are not contrary to a Compass of Right.

Life: We are all given the opportunity to explore it and maximize it if we are alive.

Hope: This is a positive sense that Better exists and that with guidance we can get there.

Right: We all know what is right or wrong for ourselves.

Desire: Instinctive energy to be satisfied, fulfilled, experience joy and peace of mind.

Selfish: Breathing and Right is better than the alternative.

Different: We are all guaranteed to be different.

Better: No one prefers Worse.

Wrong: We all know how to use it and we know it hurts ourselves and others.

Misguided: Right has more in it for us than Wrong.

Anxious: Worse as a preferred living condition is wrong.

Limited: Time to be alive on earth is not extendable.

 There are more things that we all have in common than this list. Commonalities that should bring us together when we need to or want to without fear or distrust that our own Better is a target for attack or elimination. This position has the potential to solve the discourse everywhere including our homes, our workplace, and our communities. We have witnessed success ourselves.

 If we can establish between each other our commonalities and agree that honorable Better is the only acceptable destination in all that we do, successful Better will become more common.

¤ ¤ ¤

Is Right Collectively Better?

Part Six

Applying Right

Sense Of Urgency

Your life is either in the pursuit of your Better right now or it is not. Is Better important to you? How much time do you think you have left to get to Better? Is your Better overdue? Life has a different sense of urgency when we see so much opportunity and so little time. It is not the same pressure that comes from killing ourselves to satisfy the Better of others but it is the joy of getting on the most thrilling ride ever as many times as possible before the amusement park closes.

Overdue means that we could have started using Right to our benefit earlier. Overdue can mean to act before it's too late. Overdue can be a sense that confirms that you owe a better life to yourself. Overdue means stopping what is regularly consuming your peace of mind. Overdue can mean getting trustworthy tools in the hands of our youth not yet fully ensnared by Wrong.

Overdue can mean the impact of a Better me on a Better we. Every day with wrong in the way of our Right is a day lost forever. Overdue means becoming more selfish about Right and more selfish about a fulfilled life.

Overdue may be reaching into extended levels of Better not yet achieved by those already applying Right. Our individual sense of urgency comes from the unused or overlooked ability to apply something that we all have in a way that can affect positive change quickly.

Like ourselves, a new or renewed application of Right is an opportunity for subtle course corrections, new paths, and even completely new lives realized by moving away from Wrong and Worse more consistently and with purpose.

It is never too late for "more Better", and it is never a better time to start than now.

¤ ¤ ¤

Stand Up On Purpose

Amazing things happen when we put our feet on a foundation that is right for us when we have a guidance source that will only point to Better no matter who we are, and if we use it and trust it. Cutting through the clutter of Wrong is now easier once trying and using the two simple steps of defining our Better and checking with our Compass of Right regularly.

What happens is a real sense of breaking away from our reliance on Wrong and our escaping the conditions of Worse. It is the same sensation of getting off our knees after being held there by oppression of any or all kinds. Our Better and Right give us the trust and confidence needed to get off our knees.

The condition of being forced onto our knees occurs when we move through life with the perspective or reality of a burdened life instead of the desire to pursue and achieve satisfaction and joy. We can even have so much weight from Worse, Wrong, and regrets that we are forced to crawl through our day. Being content on our knees is not natural. When you were a toddler, you burned with a desire to stand up. Remember? Okay, maybe you don't remember...

However, standing is instinctive and comes with the expectation of seeking Better. No one teaches this. We just know it. It is in our welcome package.

Better is out there once we stand up physically or figuratively to see above Worse. Worse just isn't right. Let's get going.

¤ ¤ ¤

Full Contact Sport

As we apply Right in the real world we can expect contact and conversations with others that may get bumpy. Being in motion is a lot of what we do in the pursuit of our Better. We are compelled to be on the move to cross paths with those we seek out, and when on the move, we encounter plenty of others without planning to. There is a lot of contact all along the way. Eye contact, talking, texting, emailing, shaking hands, bumped into.

Where we live and where we go is our playing field, and it has lots of players and lots of motion. More like football than golf. Golf is rewarding and fun but golf can always be played alone. Pursuing Better cannot be done alone. Football players are required to think constantly about what they are doing. There is always a lot going on, a lot of motion. They love to learn plays, to engage and involve others. They like to solve problems. They like to improve. They don't always like to practice.

They learn how to protect themselves. They don't fear the injuries that they know are going to hurt. They play through pain and discomfort. When on the field, they give it all they've got. They know which goal posts are theirs. Victories are earned and worthwhile. Like their game, our lives are a full contact sport.

Inspired Right.

Is this any different than a working mom with or without a husband, three kids, and a mortgage? Or a full-time student working three jobs? Or an aspiring musician? Or anyone in motion? Identical in many cases. However, there are some significant differences.

Football players always know where their goal posts are, the ones that are best for them and they never take their eyes off their goals. Much like the pursuit of Better.

¤ ¤ ¤

Love A Battlefield

Applying Right can also be highly emotional on the way to inspirational. Whenever we think of inspiration it is easy to go right to the topic of love. Becoming inspired Right is a target destination for us, but could we love the guidance of Right? Now, love is a topic all on its own relative to true love, superficial, etc., but for our purposes, if our defined Better is not inspirational it has a lesser opportunity to effect change for the better, and Better is what we enjoy most.

Things we may love that are inspirational include romance, books, theater, film, art, music, tales of woe and victory, real life underdog stories, confidence, comfort, satisfaction, better, etc. What we don't love, or don't find inspirational, are the things that are not right for us. We don't often consciously say, "That really just isn't right for me.", but we know almost right away if something is not. It's instinctive and intuitive. We don't like it. We don't love it. No discussion necessary. We just know.

This is true and possible because our skill in choosing is rooted in our knowledge of the difference between right and wrong for us.

As we encounter a potential "love" situation, the compass can be a little slow to react or to strongly pull us in a direction stimulated by our thinking or physical needs. We may have to battle ourselves, our impatience to confirm something or someone worthy of our love or to be safe to love.

Now, becoming highly skeptical and overly analytical is not the prescribed method for applying the guidance of Right. We don't want to become so cautious and paranoid that we'll miss true love in many areas of romance, our life's work, or more. We have the full authority and ability to make quick, instinctive calls on Right and Wrong or Better or Worse.

Serious decisions should be taken so with a smart application of the guidance of Right. Being wrong about loving engineering and later becoming a baker because that is a vocation you can love does not have the same scar tissue or irreversible collateral damage as becoming a single parent in error.

If new romance is not listed in your Foundation maybe there is a good reason. "If I pursue this relationship and it is true love based on trust and honesty, will I have to forgo my dream of becoming an astronaut?" or, "If we commit and children are a must-have will that forego my dream of becoming an astronaut?" or, "If we don't fully commit and children are an accident and the union never happens, will that forego my dream of becoming an astronaut?" Compass to self, "Keep your pants on. Slow down."

Simple, right? At this point, we know some people will even find this silly. The truth is if this silly drill happened more often we all could avoid a lot of pain, disappointment, poverty, slavery, victim mentalities, and regrets consistently.

More so, the opportunities in front of us all would happen more often as well. The key is being honest with ourselves, falling in love with Right, and not feeling guilty about being life selfish.

¤ ¤ ¤

Money Mercenary

Using our sense of Right when money is involved can be tricky. Part of every journey in America has a component of cash in the story or the formula. Is cash an enabler or a destination? Is it a measuring stick along the way? If so, quantify rich, richer, richest. How about quantifying full, fuller, fullest. Bet we'd be better at quantifying broke, broker, broker still. Money can't buy you love. Some would say, "Wanna bet?"

More to the point, and our only intention here, is to bring to the table debt and not the circular conversation around how much is enough. More pursuits to Better are interrupted by debt or single parenting than just about any other obstacle. Debt forces us to take jobs we don't love and single parent homes force us to put our lives entirely on hold to raise a child.

For now, let's apply the Compass of Right to the topic of debt, not to be considered different than credit because for most today they are one in the same.

By better applying the guidance of Right to financial decisions it is almost 100% guaranteed that you will not become enslaved or indentured to the pursuit of paper money.

Not to steal from Nancy Reagan, but when it comes to unnecessary purchases "just say no!" Credit debt is a drug, or as addictive as a drug, particularly when you have little or no cash. Or you are addicted to the image that you think you project by overspending on stuff you don't need or you cannot afford. So, apply the same thinking as not becoming enslaved by drugs. Just say no to debt. Credit is debt.

Debt is enslavement in credit's clothing. If you don't say no and take on another credit card or payday loan or car note or second or third mortgage is that a reflection of your lack of willpower or lack of financial savvy? Maybe it is. More likely, it only points out that you have not yet gotten serious about what is right for you.

The misery of indebtedness is not Better for anyone. Going forward, ask yourself one simple question, "Is this debt going to enable me or disable me from moving towards better?"

¤ ¤ ¤

One Piece Of Paper

Now that we've shared a few application examples, let's get organized and mobilized towards Better. Your initial investment will require one piece of paper and a dose of honesty. At the top, we set up three columns that are the key aspects of our lives where Better exists and where Worse and Wrong should come out.

This is the start of your own personal, confidential Foundation for Better. You can refer to this or just use it for this exercise. Some of us have used the same piece of paper since day one and update it as we arrive at our Better(s) and pick new ones to pursue.

"Foundation for Better" Worksheet

Home	Work	Social
1	1	1
2	2	2
3	3	3

List Your New Or Overdue Targets For Better and Existing Conditions of Worse or Wrong In Each Column

Foundation

The principles that you choose to subscribe to at home, work, and in the community socially are the foundations you stand on. Within these segments of our lives we have conditions of better or worse. Better than where I am now or worse than where I want to be. By identifying each area within these three groupings and an associated goal of what Better should look like is how to establish a Foundation for Better.

For example, at home my compass tells me that I should be more attentive. Being or appearing to be disengaged with my family is wrong because it leaves me dissatisfied. Being more attentive is better for me. On my list, I add "Attentive". Foundationally, when I am more attentive consistently my Better becomes a reality. It more than likely becomes a reality for my family as well.

Until it does become a reality, my list is a reminder every day where I need to pay close attention to my compass. In every conversation or situation at home I am thinking about how to be more attentive and asking my compass to show me the way. More examples are available as you read ahead.

¤ ¤ ¤

Defining Your Better

What goes on your foundational list, a list that can change over time as your seasons in life do, should be verified by your sense of Right first. Is the goal of being more attentive at home, from the example on the previous page, right for me? If it isn't then don't add it. Once we start to define one goal or target for Better we will start to see more areas emerge that are either obvious or not so obvious including decisions not yet made or topics where confusion about direction persists.

Better becomes less vague and more realistic if Better is not a "one size fits all" concept. "I want a better life at home.", is vague. As the failures of most projects or goals in life result from a lack of definition, if you pursue Better and the goal is vague, you can expect the same outcome of falling short and being disappointed.

"What if I am not sure about the specifics of my Better?", is also a common question. Just knowing that home is not vibrant or a fully alive experience is a start. Questions and conversations with others at home can help. Do they see the same things you do or are they feeling the same sense of disappointment?

Approaching the conversation with the specific goal of Better in mind, and trusting your compass along the way is an easy way to get started. Start slow and small unless there is a huge issue in your face that needs immediate attention.

How you define your Better on your worksheet is to start to identify areas in your home, at work, and socially where Better might be possible or you know you are using Wrong to get what you want or you are stuck in the condition of Worse.

From our experience with this exercise, you may see commonality across the columns. For example, a Better outcome from new honesty has a likelihood of being impactful at home, at work or elsewhere. These patterns are helpful when prioritizing what to focus on and when.

¤ ¤ ¤

Destination Alive

We think of our Betters as destinations. It's where we want to go and where we want to stay. In our last years, we are prone to look back and reflect on where we have been and what we have done. Did I waste my life? Did I have a good life? Essentially, this means that we don't know. We don't know if our lives were better or worse for us personally because we never defined our objectives or destinations.

There is no need for this to be a mystery. This time of reflection can happen with very little time left on the clock or every day when trapped in Worse. When thinking about this question, did we feel remorseful, regretful, ashamed without the ability to say for certain why? This is common without a defined foundation and the right guidance, or living without a real sense or interest in the opportunity.

First, if you do not see value in the simple existence of your life you can never know if you wasted it or not. Wasting is mismanaging something that has some form of value. If you do not see or know that your presence has value, then defining your Better can be a great way to see what you have been missing.

The exercise of defining Better is proving to possess the ability to uncover hidden value and inspirational destinations away from Wrong and Worse for everyone, including the apathetic and the directionless.

Being keenly alive is a destination that your Compass of Right is locked in on at all times. If you pay attention to it you will find that it points in the complete opposite direction of Wrong and Worse every single time. Use it, and you will know exactly where your life is all the time and the gaps you can fill with more of your Better.

Relying on the guidance of Right instead of exercising the tactics of Wrong can be the difference between being keenly alive or being among the walking dead. The walking dead are the first to find life to be a burden and to have the highest levels of dissatisfaction in most or all areas of their day.

The walking dead are not necessarily mute and without emotion or daily life participation. The walking dead do not only live on skid row. The walking dead includes the seemingly successful and prominent. For all, the persona and the unavoidable negative energy and pressure that comes from the burden of Worse is real and constant inside us and not always externally evident. We speak from our own experiences while away from Right.

Choices were made to end up on the treadmill of the walking dead and choices impact being more fully alive.

Inspired Right.

Our choices are not always thought through carefully but we are influenced by what we know and who influences us or had influenced us when we were younger.

If what we know does not include an understanding of the priority of honorable Better, we have a high probability of treadmill living. We will make concessions and give up on our Better without much thought or resistance.

¤ ¤ ¤

Fill Not Fix

Better is a simple replacement strategy. Replace Wrong and Worse with Right and Better. When we fill our thoughts, decisions, and actions with the priority of Better and rely on our Compass of Right for guidance there is less and less room to harbor Wrong and Worse. Also, going backwards to fix our pasts with a new application of Right is not always required as a condition of moving forward. Keep this in mind as you build your foundation and live it every day going forward.

Maybe we had some spots where we didn't rely on Right earlier and sense that we can go backwards and fix it, make it better. Maybe we had some spots that we now regret where we took advantage of someone and think we can go backwards and fix it, make them better. Maybe we had Better right in front of us and didn't see it at the time and think we can go back and start over.

Let us say that unscrambling eggs is not easy, and in many cases, not worth the effort. Sometimes you must simply throw out the screwed-up omelets and start over. The pursuit of Better is a forward motion activity.

Replacing Wrong is a forward motion activity. Getting out of Worse is a forward motion activity. Forward motion is satisfying.

Standing still or falling backwards to try to fix the past is neither positive motion or guaranteed to be satisfying.

Look, we all come to this party with baggage. Our foundations may have been suspect, our guidance many times was wrong, our ability to not get trapped in Worse was weak, our rationalizations justifying Wrong were expert, and a lot of damage may have been done. The wrongs committed were not right for us.

Honesty and sincere apologies go a long way. The time required to heal wounds can be most productive when used to look ahead to your newly defined Better and honorably, rightfully pursuing it. Move ahead. Keep filling yourself and your day with Better and Right and there won't be anything left to fix.

¤ ¤ ¤

Better Home

Defining our Better began by considering the condition of our homes. Beginning your list on "Home" column may not be the order that you choose, but we started here because for some of us home is where we wanted Better right away, and home is where a lot of our attention for positive change needed to be.

"Home" is not necessarily a building. Home is where our personal relationships reside, where we nourish our health and well-being, where we decide how we use our money and our finances, where we rest, where we are intimate, where we come back to every day after our pursuits and reflect on our progress in the pursuit of Better.

Home as a starting point also made sense because getting started with a new understanding of the guidance of Right in the pursuit of our Better can be a very personal step or process.

Most things personal happen at home or come from influences at home. It can be more comfortable defining our Betters and trying the application of Right first at home. Applying Right at home helped us see other opportunities and potentials for successful Betters elsewhere as we applied the guidance of Right and saw new opportunities for satisfaction materialize.

Starting at home helped us to build confidence in our use of the guidance of Right.

To get started, ask yourself and answer a few questions. "Is my home life better or worse than I want it to be?", "Where do I see the potential for Better or where do I want Better at home?". This list should only include those things or areas where you want Better for yourself. Better for others comes later.

For example, Better for me may be to get out of debt; feel better physically; pay attention more; listen better; argue less; focus on Better; get someone out of my life; get someone into my life; speak with more kindness; find someone else focusing on Better, etc.

For some of us, this list is short, for others, it is longer. This list will change over time as your life moves on. It may change even as you think more and apply your sense of Right.

The one requirement for a true foundation capable of supporting wherever your Better may be is personal honesty. Without being honest with ourselves first, this exercise and a pursuit of Better will be meaningless.

¤ ¤ ¤

Better Work

The workplace can be a daunting environment when first applying the guidance of Right. So much of our work management and guidance relies on the acceptance and promotion of Wrong. For those who work in the home as parents, mentors, or guardians, extending or teaching the guidance of Right can be equally daunting if you don't have your Right correct first.

Defining your Better work, your life's work or vocation is no different than the process of defining your Better home. The beauty and excitement about becoming reliant on the guidance of Right are that is crosses all borders and knows no boundaries in our lives. As you read more about your Better and your Right, you will see that no other source of guidance is as steady, reliable, and trustworthy in all we do. You may begin to wonder why we go out of our way to ignore the guidance of Right in the first place.

At work, or in our chosen vocations, settling for Worse is a common and consistent source of anxiousness, anxiety, and dissatisfaction. Work is the dominant consumer of our time and energy, and we consistently settle for jobs or roles that do not support our Better in any way other than a source of some level of income.

Inspired Right.

Depending on your age or career stage today, moving away from Worse work may not make sense or may be impractical.

At the same time, applying the guidance of Right can improve your work day and co-worker relations in new ways. Begin to define your Better work targets on your sheet of paper by asking yourself and answering a few questions. "Is my work life better or worse than I want it to be?", "Where do I want Better at work?", "Am I pursuing my life's work?".

Your life's work is what inspires you. It is what has the best opportunity to satisfy you. Most people say no to the last question. Our cultural and personal acceptance of Worse at work is an extension of our habit of settling for Worse elsewhere in our lives and vice versa.

Relying on the guidance of Right to identify and pursue your preferred life's work is a great place to begin to break the cycle of accepting Worse. Demonstrating the guidance of Right in the workplace can also break the cycle of actively promoting Wrong.

¤ ¤ ¤

Better Social

For our communities to become inclusive and more accepting, we must all agree that Better is the only objective in all we do. The only way to verify the objectives and intentions of others is to determine if Right guides them, or if they are addicted to Wrong.

If any leadership person or group cannot demonstrate a knowledge of the guidance of Right, or show that their majority commits to an honorable pursuit of Better, they should not be trusted to participate in your pursuit of Better.

That paragraph may sound a little militant, and it is if you want to defend or promote Worse and Wrong. As individuals, if we can focus on defining our own honorable Betters, and improve our ability to demonstrate the use of the guidance of Right, a trustworthy base of people and citizens will emerge.

Our feelings and observations tell us that much of the socially and politically militant and angry activities today are mostly desperate cries for help to find simple, trustworthy common ground.

If you remember, one size does not fit all in Better. What does fit all is access to the trustworthy guidance of Right. Not political Right or self-righteous Right. Simple, honest, undeniable Right. If something is not right for you it is simply wrong.

Our goal is to help each reader build the confidence needed to stand on a personal foundation for Better without needing to be negatively militant or to throw rocks on the way to satisfaction.

Now begin to list your community hobbies, social activities, schools, sports, civic, political, and faith groups, social media, and all things digital. "Are these groups or environments relying on the guidance of Right or contributing to the pursuit of my Better?" Remember, your Better first.

"Where in these community or social areas do I want Better?", "Where can my Better be seen or more useful in my community or social areas?", "Where can I try the guidance of Right in my community and social areas as I pursue my Better?".

The piece of paper you started now should list what shapes a beginning foundation for your Better home, Better work, and Better community. Defining your Better is a great starting point, and simple, right?

See, knowing your Better is easy if you've been honest with yourself. Using Right only builds your confidence about Better. Any surprises so far in defining your Better?

¤ ¤ ¤

Right Confidence

Did you ever do something for the first time that you wanted to do or needed to do and didn't have any real or direct experience going in? You should then be familiar with the uneasiness that comes with an initial lack of confidence. Uneasiness is normal.

You don't necessarily know what to expect completely and uncertainty can either be a momentary bout of queasy or paralyzing. Some find this experience to be an exciting part of the adventure; others find uncertainty to be terrifying. A pursuit of new Better can be both!

Defining your Better for the first time on purpose and applying the Compass of Right in live situations for the first time is no different than other new experience. The same queasy on the first day of school, new job, first date, becoming a parent, agreeing to try anchovies. Better as a formal life strategy is going to be new. Even if you've already used your instincts well, applying the Compass of Right across your life will have newness.

We cannot tell you what to completely expect from your initial or ongoing experiences with your Better. For some of us the targets of Better were straight forward and the guidance of Right quickly became second nature.

Some expected a pedestrian process and experienced a Better at life shaking levels. Some of us experienced completely different sensations when pursuing our Better at home and then taking it to work and our social lives.

The honorable pursuit of your Better can be expected to be full of surprises. Doesn't that sound like life or life as it should be? In fact, the more open we are in trusting this inner guidance system the more our previously unseen doors to Better present themselves. Doors now open in areas of our lives where we may have kept them closed without an earlier desire for our Better.

Honorably pursuing your Better will require a confidence level over time above where it probably is today if your Better with definition is something new either slightly or completely. Be calm and steady as you go. Your Better is a foundation trustworthy to stand on. You built it. And Right gives you a healthy confidence to get started and to keep going.

¤ ¤ ¤

Target Rich

Ever attend an event where hors d'oeuvres were being passed around? If you were at a good one, there was a lot of variety. What made you pick one up and pop it into your mouth? The color, shape, size, arrangement or familiarity? Maybe because it was completely foreign to anything you'd eaten before and you have a natural interest in being surprised. New things are fun.

Most hors d'oeuvres are not an automatic correct guess as to their ingredients or taste. Did that ever stop you from picking it up? Maybe yes for the picky eater, but for the rest of us we pick it up and hope we don't have to find a way to elegantly spit it out. Free samples, right? Even in the stores today in the food section, free samples.

Do we have to be accomplished chefs to understand what is in the ingredients before we try it? Do we have to have someone else taste it to make sure it's not poisoned before we try it? Is it a complicated analysis process before we decide to get into motion or are we only hungry, curious, or doing what you should do when free samples are passed around? And what happens when you taste a splendid one? You want more.

Beginning to become inspired Right is very much like a cocktail party with a lot of unidentifiable, free sample hors d'oeuvres being passed around just dying to be picked up and tasted.

Think instead that Better and the application of Right are plentiful, free sample opportunities at home, the workplace and in the community. Where we could grab one opportunity and apply some Right to it before over analyzing and talking ourselves out of Better.

Free target samples capable of being a part of a new Better worthy of receiving the attention of Right are everywhere. Applying Right does not have to be an elaborate strategy to begin with. Just implement it into small, simple or random things or needs that are in motion around you. In our key or major life applications of Right on your foundational list more thought and process may be required.

For many other circumstances and opportunities, the rapid application of Right is fun and easy. What's stopping you from trying?

¤¤¤

Step Out

We've made a lot of references to motion because we cannot get to any of our Better by standing still. Get off your knees. Stand up. Move forward. Move away from Wrong and Worse. Follow your compass. Go after Better more. In preparation of motion, we introduced a simple way to define your Foundation of Better. Your foundation is essentially your map with the destinations ahead that are right or better for you.

So, step out and get your Better! You may know enough new or are inspired by the idea of Right now to do exactly that. We did the same thing at one point. We didn't have all the discoveries that we now know that can help to anticipate obstructions in our paths and how to move with more speed and confidence away from Wrong. We did it the hard way, which wasn't really hard at all when we trusted our Right.

We also didn't completely understand our addictions to Wrong and why we were so comfortable with Worse. There are strong even formidable forces out there that will not understand your Better at first, if at all, and they may want to slow you down, discourage you, keep you trapped, or stop you from moving ahead altogether. You can expect little encouragement from others at first unless you are in the presence of other Betters.

So, step out with Right in hand and keep formulating your Foundation for Better. Always remember to start your day with a focus and appreciation for your Better and the gift of life and to come home and reflect on the progress towards your Better and the positive change taking root in yourself and those who you encounter Better.

It is no longer a crime to be happy. In fact, it was never a crime to be happy or satisfied to the level of joy. Those who want to take advantage of us are happy to trap us in Worse and those who enjoy being there love to have company.

¤ ¤ ¤

A Hand Up

Have you ever encountered a person who had life nailed from their perspective and they couldn't resist making sure that you knew all about it? How about someone like that who then expected agreement and adoption of what they were saying because anyone who did otherwise was going to be made to feel stupid?

In this case, we are not just talking about religious or political zealots. It's easy to become self-righteous once mastering our own Right. We touch on this because being self-righteous is not necessary, is counterproductive in getting to Better once Right selfish or life selfish. If we become self-righteous, we've stepped off our Foundation for Better and are going in the direction of Wrong.

Remember, what is Right or Better for you may not be for others. What is Right for others may not be Right for you. You should resist their agenda as well as they will resist yours if the goal is not Better. Ultimately, Right and Better bring us all to the same place, common ground. But how you get there is based only on what's Better for you. How you stay there is what makes you honorable.

Some will want to talk about their new found understanding of Better or their mastery of Right. Some may want to shout with glee.

Just remember that not everyone is going to know about the inspiration or the opportunity of Right when we are ready to ring the bell.

With the new or renewed confidence that will come from taking control of one's life and pursuing Better, there will be more and more opportunities to give others a hand up. The resources we have will be squandered less often. The income and the resources we earn can grow when not bogged down in Worse.

The lifestyles we know are Better put us in a new position to help others without negatively burdening ourselves or our families. Some will see this and want to know your secret. Some will not have any way to know that different or Better is taking place in your life even if it is.

Each time lives cross your path you will have new opportunities to live positive impact. There is a big difference between the slap of condemnation from a zealot and the hand of reconciliation done Right.

The Compass of Right will allow us to reconcile with ourselves, reconcile conflicts at home and work, and to assist others to reconcile what is necessary to get on their own path to Better.

¤ ¤ ¤

Can You Stand On Better?

Part Seven

More About Right

Simply Wanting Better

Main Street Pilot is a group of friends and colleagues who had reached the top of our frustration in being able to help others get to better lives. Our group was always well intentioned and thought we had a good sense of doing the right thing.

The work we had committed to in the community and professionally to give what we could of ourselves to others in the pursuit of Better had spanned decades. Yet evidence of effectively helping others get to Better was less and less visible as the result of our direct efforts.

Getting to Better personally or collectively requires communication and openness to discussion or new ideas with others. There must be some level of trust achieved between two people in the discussion, or a person and a group, or two or more groups before Better can even start to have a chance of success.

The cultural conditions of honest and open discussion across our physical and digital main streets had essentially evaporated and Better was fading as a thing of the past. Wholesale distrust and anger now rule the day.

Inspired Right.

Then something amazing happened during a conversation with some local homeless people as we were discussing finding Better.

What happened was a realization that we had a lot more in common with people, even those wildly different than ourselves, than we ever thought until we explored Right. We also saw opportunities to use it in common, useful ways of communication to both of our advantages. How we communicated was changing.

Whenever change is in the conversation and there are two sides that are not seeing the other side clearly there is a distinct and essential need to find common ground as quickly as we can if success in small or big ways can ever be possible.

Our amazing discovery is that we all have in common, to a very high degree, is that we all know the difference between right and wrong. Forget about the many possible definitions of right or wrong for a minute. The reality is that we all have an inner sense of Right and that this sense is a condition of what is right for us individually.

However, "Right" for us personally is a common sense that we all have. A sense that we determine and can all trust because it is our own. A unique yet common ground that protects our individuality.

It doesn't matter how our group of marginal geniuses came to this conclusion. What does matter is what happened next.

We asked some questions and decided to try some things out to improve our personal and collective pursuit of Better. Personal "Right" in our culture had a bad rap for selfishness and doing the right thing is very commonly understood to be a nice conversation and not necessarily impactful or useful.

This to say that we had no expectations in our exploration into Right or any idea of what it could mean to anyone. After a lot of trial and error over about a two-year period we discovered and can now confirm that Right is not only common ground that is misunderstood and underutilized it can inspire us in new ways when we rely on the guidance it has been giving us all along.

¤ ¤ ¤

Stand Up Not Out

Where we are today in our group is not where we began. This conversation about Better and applying the guidance of Right to our lives took shape. At that time, much of what is in this book and many of the specific topics we touch on throughout were just fragments. Each of us had our own deal coming to the Right party.

Married, single, children, empty nest, more paper dollars, fewer paper dollars, energized, depressed, drifting, moving with some purpose, beginning of careers, end of careers, restarting careers, rested, tired, and other combinations made up our Today.

We had a common interest in Better for our situations and on our own terms, but the thought of getting specific, mapping out the issues and finding a solution, if possible, for a Better today came about through trial and error. We had to try Right - a lot.

A common thread beyond the common ground presented throughout the book was a defined or loosely defined interest in a better America. Some within our group are veterans, even combat veterans. Each of us has served in civic organizations or even led public initiatives fueled by wanting Better beyond ourselves.

At the beginning of this journey, we were only able to restate the obvious problems until we arrived at the foundation of the original Right. We could finally get clarity around many common problems in our communities, particularly divisiveness and apathy.

Our interest in a better America was how we collectively organized our thinking at first, but ultimately resulted in the validity of applying Right in a selfish approach with the only true goal becoming a better Today. Ironically, although stated differently elsewhere and earlier in our history, this is the same objective at the root of America's beginnings with individual Right as a clearly stated foundation.

Taxation without representation. Religious freedoms. For the people, by the people. Freedom of speech. Freedom of thought. No debtor prisons. Like nothing else on earth. Wanting Better as a group, as a territory, as a state, as a nation. But at the core it was better for us as an individual.

Wide open spaces fields of play ahead for a young country. But our habits followed from other lands and earlier times, and coagulation into divisiveness began once again around familiar or safety in numbers. The country took shape and a direction that led to groups of thinkers being redefined and not universal or new, original thought.

Groups of cultures closing ranks for isolation and protection and not openness, discovery, and learning with honest objectivity.

Land grabs and opportunity that could only be measured by things that could be counted and not by fulfillment. Yet our spirit to stand on our own persevered. We still have that spirit. We think every person deep down has that spirit. We just needed a little help in bringing the understanding of individually standing up through the malaise of our Today to see the path.

This core philosophy of standing on our own as people and not just as a government was reflected in our fight to claim an Independence Day, the standard practice and pride associated with pulling ourselves up by our bootstraps, our willingness and assumption that the only way to stand on our own was to roll up our sleeves and dig in.

In all this everyone had their own vision of Better. Moral codes existed that may not have been applied as our inner sense of Right, but the spirit of Right existed.
Today, our group wanted to stand up on our own in the spirit of our forefathers and the creator responsible for the welcome package to life that we all receive before our first breath. When we are very young and starting to grow, mobility is an instinctive skill to develop, but nothing began to happen until we could stand up.

We might not remember the first time we could see above the carpet threads all on our own, but we all have probably witnessed a baby becoming a toddler and what that means to them. It's on their face. Maybe a little fear and trepidation, but more dominantly excitement and joy.

Took some work to stand up, but the clearer vision ahead is worth it. The options displayed in our peripheral vision are new, and the need to explore is overwhelming. The look to an adult or older sibling to hold our hands until we could steady ourselves. The unshakable desire to fulfill ourselves while taking joy in pleasing our parents as well.

Is that experience, that joy, that wonderment, that never-ending motion over once we can speak, understand, and start to fill ourselves with tar, vomit, or lava? It is if we stand idly by. The joy of standing up for the first time, or throughout our lives when getting off our knees by shedding the weight of Wrong, is what the pursuit of Better is all about.

We stand up to see our horizons and opportunities that line up with who we truly are and do that so much more accurately when relying on the Compass of Right. On the other hand, we do not stand up for the sole purpose of standing out.

Inspired Right.

The competitive spirit is a factor of survival. A sense of urgency to pay attention to sustenance, to shelter, to non-extinction. This feeling of urgency can be as strong as the superhuman strength needed to lift a car off oneself or another when pinned underneath.

We all have a sense of urgency to survive, and we are all naturally selfish about it. And we continue to misdirect and abuse this competitive spirit even during our times of great knowledge, advancements in applicable science, and global information sharing.

What holds us back from Better, we feel, is a lack of an acknowledged, universal, undeniable point of reference that only points to Better. Right is that point of reference.

The foundation of the original Right is not merely a new rule book or a new coat of paint on law and order. Right is the one common ground that can have us aligning ourselves while helping each other align. This is the legitimate pursuit of Better for individuals and groups.

For those who refuse to acknowledge that Right is better, it is only a matter of time before the individuals committed to Right becomes a formidable force guided by the same compass, the new honorable majority. A majority of individuals.

It began for us as we decided that we truly wanted Better and decided to stand up. Stand up newly on a foundational truth that has eliminated militant anger and the fear of different.

We have not sacrificed our personal convictions, our relational interests, our chosen career paths, or our interest in enjoying the sustenance, shelter and delicious hors d'oeuvre surprises that we know are on our path to Better.

As we further our commitment to better applying the guidance of Right individually, we are also committed to introducing this book and concept as broadly as possible.

Right, will no longer be an undervalued cliché once it is openly and purposely put into use more widely over time. We are selfish about standing up in America. We are selfish about standing on our own Foundation for Better.

We are not standing against any one or any group. We are standing against Wrong and the unnecessary condition of Worse.

¤ ¤ ¤

What Defines You?

Notes

Right Questions

Compass Point questions. Just fill in the blank. "Is……. Right or Wrong for me?"

- ¤ Not using valuable knowledge...

- ¤ Refusing to be honest...

- ¤ Acting without thinking...

- ¤ Cheating on income taxes...

- ¤ Sharing the personal information of others...

- ¤ Destroying property because you are mad...

- ¤ Supporting the destruction of another life...

- ¤ Betraying trust...

- ¤ Deceiving others to gain an advantage...

Inspired Right.

Notes

Right Questions

Compass Point questions. Just fill in the blank. "Is……. Right or Wrong for me?"

- Not going to work when you can...
- Not finishing a task important to others...
- Not finishing a task important to you...
- Plagiarism or copying the work of others...
- Plagiarizing your work to cut corners...
- Openly disrespecting others...
- Openly disrespecting yourself...
- Secretly disrespecting others...
- Openly disrespecting others...
- Repeating something that may or may not be true...

Inspired Right.

Notes

Right Questions

Compass Point questions. Just fill in the blank. "Is....... Right or Wrong for me?"

- Getting mad because you don't understand...

- Taking anger out on others...

- Spending time on meaningless endeavors...

- Dreaming about Better...

- Acting upon Better...

- Complaining about not having Better...

- Not disclosing a bad engine when selling a car...

- Throwing away food...

- Being inspired by Right...

Notes

Right Questions

Compass Point questions. Just fill in the blank. "Is....... Right or Wrong for me?"

- Taking off clothes to win affection...
- Hoping that others will mentor your children...
- Using children as pawns...
- Feeling sorry for oneself...
- Not experiencing new things...
- Living without a budget...
- Turning the other cheek...
- Staying in an abusive relationship...
- Leaving mentoring of children to someone else...
- Remaining uninspired...

Notes

Better Questions

Compass Point questions. Just fill in the blank. "Is……. Better or Worse for me?"

- ¤ No chosen direction…
- ¤ No directional compass…
- ¤ No interests…
- ¤ Too many interests…
- ¤ Not trusting others…
- ¤ Trusting others automatically…
- ¤ Waiting for the right person…
- ¤ Not seeking the right person…
- ¤ Committing to the wrong person…

Inspired Right.

Notes

Better Questions

Compass Point questions. Just fill in the blank. "Is……. Better or Worse for me?"

- Lusting instead of intimacy...

- Intimacy instead of lust...

- Normal health...

- Debt in support of your Better...

- No goals...

- Too many goals...

- No unnecessary debt...

- Standing firm on desires and interests...

- Compromising your Better...

Inspired Right.

Notes

Better Questions

Compass Point questions. Just fill in the blank. "Is....... Better or Worse for me?"

- A white lie...

- Lacking confidence to communicate...

- Stingy with time...

- Stingy with money...

- Multiple cars...

- Multiple houses...

- Girlfriend or boyfriend on the side...

- Faking credentials...

- Over stimulation...

- Pornography as art...

- Hiding a problem...

Inspired Right.

Notes

Keys To Better Success

Snapshot list of reminders that improve our opportunity for success in an honorable pursuit of Better.

Top 12

- The origin of our sense of Right relates us all.
- Right for you is your foundation.
- Become selfish about Right for you.
- Right selfish eliminates future regrets.
- Become selfish about moving away from Wrong.
- Better for you should not prey on others.
- Right will show you better paths and keep you there.
- Standing on Right is easier with the right compass.
- Help others understand what Right has in it for them.
- Honor those who acknowledge Right.
- Never forget that we all share Right.
- The compass of Right should be used at all times.

Right Your Book

This is a play on words but this is the opportunity within us all. To write our own book and chronicle our pursuit and success with Better. We become a live sighting of Better. Like any book read for the first time, there are surprises and the story can go in a new direction without notice. Life is exciting like that too when lived with a sense of being keenly alive.

We suggest you keep your eyes open and tune your Compass as you look forward to Better in all that you do. The beginnings of your Foundation for Better should be helping you already if you've gotten started. Achieve Better for yourself by hearing your spouse. Achieve Better for yourself by simplifying ethics at work.

Achieve Better for yourself by exercising kindness in social media. Achieve Better for yourself by no longer settling for Worse or relying on an addiction to Wrong. Right and Better, just like your life, are all about you.

You will find selected list options on the following pages can help to start formulating your targets and fine tuning your Foundation for Better. An idea is not an idea until you put it in writing!

¤ ¤ ¤

Inspired Right.

Is Anger Better For You?

Wrong Tactics To Right

1

2

3

4

5

Think about where Wrong is used and where Right could replace it.

Where Is Your Better?

People To Approach Better

1

2

3

4

5

Think about new acquaintances, strangers, or people you know where Wrong can be removed from your approach.

Can You Build On Right?

Ideas For Life's Work

1

2

3

4

5

Think about what you need to satisfy or inspire you within your job either inside or outside of the home.

Inspired Right.

Can You Be Selfish For Right?

Traits Of Right Mate

1

2

3

4

5

Think about what you would find most compatible or essential in the character or traits of those that will fill your relationship Better.

Have Too Much Better?

Ideas For Personal Better

1

2

3

4

5

Think about your earlier Foundation for Better ideas and consider adding more areas or targets where better would be great for you.

Inspired Right.

Can Right Be Addictive?

Ideas For Professional Better

1

2

3

4

5

You may have maxed out your ideas for professional Better on your Foundation for Better. Are there more areas or targets where better would be great for you?

Inspired Right.

What Steals Your Peace?

Ideas For Civic Better

1

2

3

4

5

Think about areas or targets in your social or community life where opportunities for Better may be. It is okay to be fearless and chart new territory!

Inspired Right.

Right Our Next Book

If the application of Right changes your life or accelerates your Better in small amazing ways or huge life shaking ways, we'd love to hear about it if you would like to share. We'll keep your credentials confidential if you choose. Our website is a good place to let us know.

Our intention is to share successes and challenges from the real world in our future books, our speaking engagements, our workplace working sessions and anywhere else a good story can emphasize the possibility and the joy untapped and released from within us all.

www.MainStreetPilot.com

Inspired Right

A Better Movement

One Better at a time. With a broad acknowledgment and prioritization of the guidance of Right every person and community in the world can speak the same language and share the exact objectives that are based on provable trust and Better.

¤ ¤ ¤

Inspired Right.

Is A Better Me A Better We?

Inspired Speakers

Our team can provide direct experience of better applying the guidance of Right, along with over seventy-five years of combined experience in family, business and government personal, professional, and leadership development expertise to any event where thought-provoking, motivational and inspirational content is required. Please contact us for the facilitation of your class or working group sessions or programs on the foundational elements of the original Right, how to organize, prepare and execute with the compass of Right as a tool and a guide.

Inspired Programs

Program materials organized to introduce, understand and apply the core concepts and topics outlined in Inspired Right. Simply better for everyone. Single topic or programs of developmental curricula are available to include Becoming Inspired Right™, Right Selfish™, Life Selfish™, Wrongaholics Anonymous™, Mentoring Right™, Executing Right™, and more. Multi-language and cultural specific content available.

Inspired Right.

Inspired Content

Our content is available for integration into your internal or commercial programs, and for private labeling or branding to complement personal, professional, and leadership improvement or development professionals and human capital management executives. Our content is suited for group and organizational applications including church programs, commercial programs including ethics effectiveness and the right way to engineer and operate companies and more. Multi-language and cultural specific content available.

And More

Please look forward to more compelling books and publications from Main Street Pilot as we fully optimize applying the guidance or Right in all we do.

Is Your Right Inspirational?

Who's Responsible For Your Better?

Your Better Is All About You

- *Peace* -

CPSIA information can be obtained
at www.ICGtesting.com
Printed in the USA
FSOW02n0737281216
28918FS